KU-414-473

Contents

Corgi Modern Poets
In Focus: 4

Edited by

Jeremy Robson

CORGI BOOKS
TRANSWORLD PUBLISHERS LTD
A National General Company

CORGI MODERN POETS IN FOCUS: 4

A CORGI BOOK 0 552 08844 7

First publication in Great Britain

PRINTING HISTORY
Corgi edition published 1971

Introductions and selection © Jeremy Robson, 1971
Acknowledgments for the use of copyright material will be
found on page 8 which is hereby made part of this copyright
page.

Corgi Books are published by Transworld
Publishers Ltd.,
Cavendish House, 57-59 Uxbridge Road,
Ealing, London W.5

Made and printed in Great Britain by
Cox & Wyman Ltd., London, Reading and Fakenham

DANIEL HOFFMAN

ACKNOWLEDGMENTS

For poems by Thomas Hardy from *Collected Poems* to the Trustees of the Hardy Estate, the Macmillan Company of Canada and Macmillan London and Basingstoke. For poems by Dannie Abse, to the author for 'A New Diary', 'Miss Book World', 'No More Mozart' and 'Forgotten'; to Hutchinson and Co. for 'Anniversary', 'Return to Cardiff', 'Chalk', 'Pathology of Colours', 'The Water Diviner', 'As I Was Saying', 'Interview With a Spirit Healer' and 'Hunt the Thimble' from *Selected Poems* (1970). For Poems by Vernon Scannell, to the author for 'Battlefields' and 'End of a Season', and for 'The Telephone Number', 'My Father's Face', 'The Men Who Wear My Clothes', 'I'm Covered Now', 'Walking Wounded', 'Taken in Adultery', 'Death in the Lounge Bar', 'An Old Lament Renewed', and 'View From a Deck Chair' from *Selected Poems* (Allison & Busby, 1971). For poems by Stevie Smith, to her executor Mr. James MacGibbon for 'The Weak Monk' from *Harold's Leap* (Chapman & Hall, 1950), for 'Not Waving But Drowning', 'I Remember' and 'The Jungle Husband' from *Not Waving But Drowning* (André Deutsch, 1957), for 'Thoughts About a Person from Porlock' from *Selected Poems* (Longmans, 1964), for 'A House of Mercy', 'Tenuous and Precarious', and 'Oh Christianity, Christianity' from *The Frog Prince* (Longmans, 1966), and for 'O Pug', 'Scorpion' and 'Come, Death' from *Scorpion and Other Poems* (Longmans, 1971): application for the use of these or other poems by Stevie Smith should be made to Mr. MacGibbon c/o the publisher. For poems by Tony Harrison, to the author for 'The Hands' from *Earthworks* (Northern House, 1964), 'Durham' and 'Fonte Luminosa'; to London Magazine Editions and the author for 'The Nuptial Torches', 'Thomas Campey', 'Newcastle is Peru' and 'A Proper Caution' from *The Loiners* (1970). For poems by Daniel Hoffman, to the author for 'The Clams' and 'The Seals of Penobscot Bay' from *An Armada of Thirty Wales* (Yale University Press, 1953); to Oxford University Press of America for 'In the Beginning' and 'Safari' from *A Little Geste* (1960), for 'A Meeting' and 'The Pursued' from *The City of Satisfactions* (1963), for 'Moving Among the Creatures', 'Keys' and 'Last Words' from *Striking the Stones* (1968), and for 'A Special Train' from *Broken Laws* (1970). The prose piece by Dannie Abse was taken from *The Listener*. The prose statements by Vernon Scannell, James MacGibbon, Tony Harrison (originally titled 'The Inkwell of Doktor Agrippa') and Daniel Hoffman were especially written for this volume.

Corgi Modern Poets
In Focus: 4

THOMAS HARDY

THOMAS HARDY is all too often thought of as a novelist who wrote poetry as a secondary activity, more or less in his spare time. Indeed there are many readers of his novels who remain unaware that he wrote poetry at all. Yet Hardy always thought of himself as being primarily a poet; and, following the publication of *Jude The Obscure* (1895) and its generally hostile reception, he gave up prose completely, devoting the remaining years of his life to poetry. When he died in 1928, at the age of 88, he left behind a vast body of work, which was to have an enduring influence on succeeding generations of poets.

Even as perceptive a critic as Lytton Strachey considered Hardy's poetry to be a bi-product of the novels. Reviewing *Satires of Circumstance* (1914) in *The New Statesman*, he wrote: 'The originality of his poetry lies in the fact that it bears everywhere upon it the impress of a master of prose fiction. . . . It is not only in its style and feeling that this poetry reveals the novelist; it is also in its subject matter.' At the same time, however, Strachey recognized the originality and power of Hardy's poems, and was clearly disturbed by them, declaring: 'They are in fact modern as no other poems'.

To many poets writing today Hardy is actually the first of the moderns. 'Nobody has taught me anything about poetry since Thomas Hardy died', declared Ezra Pound in 1934, and his admiration has been shared by a host of very different poets, among them Robert Graves, W. H. Auden, Edmund Blunden, C. Day Lewis, Robert Frost, Philip Larkin, Vernon

Scannell, John Betjeman and D. H. Lawrence. Clearly Hardy is a poet's poet. Dylan Thomas remarked that while he thought Yeats to be the greatest living poet, Hardy was the one he loved. Vernon Scannell, in a broadcast, said that he considered the poems to be 'little quintessences of the prose books and stories, fresh in a way the prose, fine as it is, can't quite claim to be.' And on that same programme ('A Man Who Noticed Things') Philip Larkin revealed that he came to Hardy with a sense of relief at not having to jack himself up to a concept of poetry that lay outside his own life: 'Hardy not only taught one how to feel, he taught one to have confidence in what one felt.'

One criticism commonly levelled at Hardy, usually by academics, is that he wrote only a handful of good poems and that to find them one has to wade through a mass of indifferent or plainly bad verse. F. R. Leavis, an admirer of Hardy, wrote that 'his rank as a major poet rests upon a dozen poems', and that 'the main impulse behind his verse is too commonly the mere impulse to write verse.' G. S. Fraser, for his part, wrote of Hardy as 'the most uneven, as he is also the most excessively copious, of great poets.' Nevertheless, the fact remains that if one were to ask Hardy's admirers to name their favourite Hardy poems, they would produce different lists, reeling off lines that sent one scuttling to the shelves to discover a poem one had previously overlooked. Philip Larkin has gone so far as to say that he likes Hardy *because* he wrote so much, because one can read about in the 800-page Collected Poems 'and still be surprised'. For him each poem has a 'little spinal chord of thought, a little tune of its own.'

It may be that Hardy was uneven – with such a prodigious output it could hardly have been otherwise; he may have spilled on occasions into sentimentality. All the same, his character is firmly stamped on almost every line he wrote, and his rhythms and diction are unique. The openings of his poems – direct, colloquial, unadorned – lead one into the heart of a world that is entirely his. The poems, set in the Dorset where he was born and spent the greater part of his life, are rooted firmly in the soil of that part of England, and one of his great achievements was to stamp his personality over a whole region so that today it is known as 'Hardy Country'. Another was to give voice to the ordinary lives, loves, aspirations and fears of ordinary people, just as he did in his prose. He was concerned above all with human suffering, with time and its passing, with love and its shifting seasons. He faced life squarely, refusing to colour what he saw with a haze of romantic make-believe. This stoicism was a main source of strength:

> Within the common lamplit room
>   Prison my eyes and thought;
> Let dingy details crudely loom,
>   Mechanic speech be wrought:
> Too fragrant was Life's early bloom,
>   Too tart the fruit it brought!

Hardy called himself an agnostic, but one senses in 'The Oxen' a desire to believe, the poet's inability to do so made all the more poignant by the feeling of loss he so delicately conveys:

> So fair a fancy few would weave
>   In these years! Yet, I feel,
> If someone said on Christmas Eve,
>   'Come; see the oxen kneel
>
> 'In the lonely barton by yonder coomb
>   Our childhood used to know,'
> I should go with him in the gloom,
>   Hoping it might be so.

Critics have often chided Hardy for his pessimism, and

while his view of life was hardly a rosy one, he could be tender and even jocular, though the humour is always low-keyed; also he had a genuine appreciation of human values. Nor were the views expressed in his poems necessarily his own, for he adopted dramatic masks and spoke in many voices. All the same, there is no ignoring the deep sense of brooding melancholy which pervades so much of his work. It is, in Lytton Strachey's words, 'The melancholy of regretful recollection, bitter speculation of immortal longings unsatisfied. That Hardy was stung by this 'black' image which had been thrust upon him may be seen from the vigorous Apology he felt compelled to write as an introduction to his 1922 volume, *Late Lyrics and Earlier:* 'What is today, in allusions to the present author's pages, alleged to be "pessimism" is, in truth, only such "questionings" in the exploration of reality and is the first step towards the soul's betterment and the body's also'. He took up the point again in the Preface to his last, posthumous book, *Winter Moods:* 'My last volume of poems was pronounced wholly gloomy and pessimistic by reviewers – even by some of the more able class. My sense of the oddity of this verdict may be imagined when, in selecting them, I had been, as I had thought, rather too liberal in admitting flippant, not to say farcical poems in the collection.' Above all, he totally rejected the idea that he was trying to peddle a particular 'view' of life. 'No harmonious philosophy is attempted in these pages', he wrote, and the authenticity of the poems themselves speaks in his defence. He was far too concerned to record in his writing what he had seen and felt to externalize and postulate. As a man of the country he enjoyed hearing – and relating – gossip and a good story (he was born in 1840 in the Dorset village of Upper Bockhamton, the son of a master-mason); as a musician he enjoyed the sound of words used well (he could tune a violin when he was four, and often gave recitals with his father in the local villages); as an architect he liked to see things well built (he was a trained architect, worked for a while in London, then for a restorer of old churches); as a tormented husband he knew the feeling of love gone wrong (his marriage to his first wife, Emma, was not a success and they were estranged for years). These were some of the forces behind his poetry which, working on various levels, could produce poems as different in their approach as the colloquial 'The Ruined Maid', the satirical 'In Church', the elegaic 'During Wind and Rain', and the lyrically haunting 'After a Journey'.

That last poem was one of a number of deeply-felt personal lyrics Hardy wrote following the death of Emma in 1912. She had been ill for some time, yet the shock of her death affected him profoundly. Although he was then 72, the voice and vision of the poem are as fresh as ever, the lyrical flow beautifully modulated and sustained throughout. It is typical of Hardy that he could turn from the sharp observation of others to give such memorable expression to the tug of his own heart, and that when he did so he drew concretely on an actual place (in this case Pentargon Bay, near Boscastle in Cornwall, where he had been called in to advise on the restoration of the church of St. Juliot), recreating it vividly together with the young girl he met there. As Hardy himself wrote in a more general context: 'I have the faculty (possibly not uncommon) for burying an emotion in my heart or brain for forty years, and exhuming it at the end of that time as fresh as when interred. For instance the poem entitled "The Breaking of Nations" contains a feeling that moved me in 1870, during the Franco-Prussian war, when I chanced to be looking at such an agricultural incident in Cornwall. But I did not write the poem till during the war with Germany of 1914.'

While Hardy may not have been an outlandish experimenter, he worked in what must be an unrivalled variety of strict verse forms, bending and extending them to suit the needs of the poem in hand. He has been called clumsy, has been said to have a poor ear. Yet his poetry is nothing if not

15

accurate, the so-called quaint phrases he throws in from time to time being precisely those one hears even today in the Dorset village pubs. Thus when he wrote 'he lipped her', he meant just that; when he began a poem ('A Countenance') with the line, 'Her laugh was not in the middle of her face quite,' the unexpected positioning of the word 'quite' not only brings the girl's face vividly to life but also catches the nuances of natural speech; when (in 'After a Journey') he wrote, 'Things were not lastly as firstly well' he telescoped into seven words the story of his wrecked marriage.

C. Day Lewis has spoken of Hardy's 'self-made manner', F. R. Leavis of his best poems being 'a triumph of character'. Here lay Hardy's strength. He entered into the life around him, took his material where and however he found it, fashioned it like the true country craftsman he was to suit his own needs. And so the phrases, rhythms and inversions which may at a first reading appear to halt a poem's progress, often turn out at a closer inspection to be the very factors which give the poet his authentic voice, enabling him not only to observe and narrate with rare accuracy, but (in Sassoon's phrase) to 'observe the semi-tones'.

THE RUINED MAID

'O 'Melia, my dear, this does everything crown!
Who could have supposed I should meet you in Town?
And whence such fair garments, such prosperi-ty?' –
'O didn't you know I'd been ruined?' said she.

– 'You left us in tatters, without shoes or socks,
Tired of digging potatoes, and spudding up docks;
And now you've gay bracelets and bright feathers three!' –
'Yes: that's how we dress when we're ruined', said she.

– 'At home in the barton you said "thee" and "thou",
And "thik oon", and "theäs oon", and "t'other"; but now
Your talking quite fits 'ee for high compa-ny!' –
'Some polish is gained with one's ruin,' said she.

– 'Your hands were like paws then, your face blue and bleak
But now I'm bewitched by your delicate cheek,
And your little gloves fit as on any la-dy!' –
'We never do work when we're ruined', said she.

– 'You used to call home-life a hag-ridden dream,
And you'd sigh, and you'd sock; but at present you seem
To know not of megrims or melancho-ly!' –
'True. One's pretty lively when ruined', said she.

– 'I wish I had feathers, a fine sweeping gown,
And a delicate face, and could strut about Town!' –
'My dear – a raw country girl, such as you be,
Cannot quite expect that. You ain't ruined', said she.

Westbourne Park Villas, 1866

SHUT OUT THAT MOON

Close up the casement, draw the blind,
   Shut out that stealing moon,
She wears too much the guise she wore
   Before our lutes were strewn
With years-deep dust, and names we read
   On a white stone were hewn.

Step not forth on the dew-dashed lawn
   To view the Lady's Chair,
Immense Orion's glittering form,
   The Less and Greater Bear:
Stay in; to such sights we were drawn
   When faded ones were fair.

Brush not the bough for midnight scents
   That come forth lingeringly,
And wake the same sweet sentiments
   They breathed to you and me
When living seemed a laugh, and love
   All it was said to be.

Within the common lamp-lit room
   Prison my eyes and thought;
Let dingy details crudely loom,
   Mechanic speech be wrought:
Too fragrant was Life's early bloom,
   Too tart the fruit it brought!

DURING WIND AND RAIN

They sing their dearest songs –
He, she, all of them – yea,
Treble and tenor and bass,
  And one to play;
With the candles mooning each face. . . .
  Ah, no; the years O!
How the sick leaves reel down in throngs!

They clear the creeping moss –
Elders and juniors – aye,
Making the pathways neat
  And the garden gay;
And they build a shady seat. . . .
  Ah, no; the years, the years;
See, the white storm-birds wing across!

They are blithely breakfasting all –
Men and maidens – yea,
Under the summer tree,
  With a glimpse of the bay,
While pet fowl come to the knee. . . .
  Ah, no; the years O!
And the rotten rose is ript from the wall.

They change to a high new house,
He, she, all of them – aye,
Clocks and carpets and chairs
  On the lawn all day,
And brightest things that are theirs. . . .
  Ah, no; the years, the years;
Down their carved names the rain-drop ploughs.

THE OXEN

Christmas Eve, and twelve of the clock.
  'Now they are all on their knees,'
An elder said as we sat in a flock
  By the embers in hearthside ease.

We pictured the meek mild creatures where
  They dwelt in their strawy pen,
Nor did it occur to one of us there
  To doubt they were kneeling then.

So fair a fancy few would weave
  In these years! Yet, I feel,
If someone said on Christmas Eve,
  'Come; see the oxen kneel

'In the lonely barton by yonder coomb
  Our childhood used to know',
I should go with him in the gloom,
  Hoping it might be so.

'I LOOK INTO MY GLASS'

I look into my glass,
And view my wasting skin,
And say, 'Would God it came to pass
My heart had shrunk as thin!'

For then, I, undistrest
By hearts grown cold to me,
Could lonely wait my endless rest
With equanimity.

But Time, to make me grieve,
Part steals, lets part abide;
And shakes this fragile frame at eve
With throbbings of noontide.

A COUNTENANCE

Her laugh was not in the middle of her face quite,
   As a gay laugh springs,
It was plain she was anxious about some things
   I could not trace quite.
Her curls were like fir-cones – piled up, brown –
   Or rather like tight-tied sheaves:
It seemed they could never be taken down. . . .

And her lips were too full, some might say:
I did not think so. Anyway,
The shadow her lower one would cast
Was green in hue whenever she passed
   Bright sun on midsummer leaves.
Alas, I knew not much of her,
And lost all sight and touch of her!

If otherwise, should I have minded
The shy laugh not in the middle of her mouth quite
And would my kisses have died of drouth quite
   As love became unblinded?

IN TIME OF 'THE BREAKING OF NATIONS'

I

Only a man harrowing clods
　In a slow silent walk
With an old horse that stumbles and nods
　Half asleep as they stalk.

II

Only thin smoke without flame
　From the heaps of couch-grass;
Yet this will go onward the same
　Though Dynasties pass.

III

Yonder a maid and her wight
　Come whispering by:
War's annals will cloud into night
　Ere their story die.

1915

AFTER A JOURNEY

Hereto I come to view a voiceless ghost;
    Whither, O whither will its whim now draw me?
Up the cliff, down, till I'm lonely, lost,
    And the unseen waters' ejaculations awe me.
Where you will next be there's no knowing,
    Facing round about me everywhere,
        With your nut-coloured hair,
And gray eyes, and rose-flush coming and going.

Yes: I have re-entered your olden haunts at last;
    Through the years, through the dead scenes I have tracked
        you;
What have you now found to say of our past –
    Scanned across the dark space wherein I have lacked you?
Summer gave us sweets, but autumn wrought division?
    Things were not lastly as firstly well
        With us twain, you tell?
But all's closed now, despite Time's derision.

I see what you are doing: you are leading me on
    To the spots we knew when we haunted here together,
The waterfall, above which the mist-bow shone
    At the then fair hour in the then fair weather,
And the cave just under, with a voice still so hollow
    That it seems to call out to me from forty years ago,
        When you were all aglow,
And not the thin ghost that I now frailly follow!

Ignorant of what there is flitting here to see,
    The waked birds preen and the seals flop lazily;
Soon you will have, Dear, to vanish from me,
    For the stars close their shutters and the dawn whitens hazily.
Trust me, I mind not, though Life lours,

The bringing me here; nay, bring me here again!
    I am just the same as when
Our days were a joy, and our paths through flowers.

AN ANCIENT TO ANCIENTS

Where once we danced, where once we sang,
     Gentlemen,
The floors are sunken, cobwebs hang,
And cracks creep; worms have fed upon
The doors. Yea, sprightlier times were then
Than now, with harps and tabrets gone,
     Gentlemen!

Where once we rowed, where once we sailed,
     Gentlemen,
And damsels took the tiller, veiled
Against too strong a stare (God wot
Their fancy, then or anywhen!)
Upon that shore we are clean forgot,
     Gentlemen!

We have lost somewhat, afar and near,
     Gentlemen,
The thinning of our ranks each year
Affords a hint we are nigh undone,
That we shall not be ever again
The marked of many, loved of one,
     Gentlemen.

In dance the polka hit our wish,
     Gentlemen,
The paced quadrille, the spry schottische,
'Sir Roger'. – And in opera spheres
The 'Girl' (the famed 'Bohemian'),
And 'Trovatore', held the ears,
     Gentlemen.

This season's paintings do not please,
     Gentlemen,

Like Etty, Mulready, Maclise;
Throbbing romance has waned and wanned;
No wizard wields the witching pen
Of Bulwer, Scott, Dumas, and Sand,
        Gentlemen.

The bower we shrined to Tennyson,
        Gentlemen,
Is roof-wrecked; damps there drip upon
Sagged seats, the creeper-nails are rust,
The spider is sole denizen;
Even she who voiced those rhymes is dust,
        Gentlemen!

We who met sunrise sanguine-souled,
        Gentlemen,
Are wearing weary. We are old;
These younger press; we feel our rout
Is imminent to Aïdes' den, –
That evening shades are stretching out,
        Gentlemen!

And yet, though ours be failing frames,
        Gentlemen,
So were some others' history names,
Who trode their track light-limbed and fast
As these youth, and not alien
From enterprise, to their long last,
        Gentlemen.

Sophocles, Plato, Socrates,
        Gentlemen,
Pythagoras, Thucydides,
Herodotus, and Homer, – yea,
Clement, Augustin, Origen,
Burnt brightlier towards their setting-day,
        Gentlemen.

And ye, red-lipped, and smooth-browed; list,
      Gentlemen;
Much is there waits you we have missed;
Much lore we leave you worth the knowing,
Much, much has lain outside our ken:
Nay, rush not: time serves: we are going,
      Gentlemen.

AFTERWARDS

When the Present has latched its postern behind my tremulous
    stay,
  And the May month flaps its glad green leaves like wings,
Delicate-filmed as new-spun silk, will the neighbours say,
  'He was a man who used to notice such things'?

If it be in the dusk when, like an eyelid's soundless blink,
  The dewfall-hawk comes crossing the shades to alight
Upon the wind-warped upland thorn, a gazer may think,
  'To him this must have been a familiar sight.'

If I pass during some nocturnal blackness, mothy and warm,
  When the hedgehog travels furtively over the lawn,
One may say, 'He strove that such innocent creatures should
    come to no harm,
  But he could do little for them; and now he is gone.'

If, when hearing that I have been stilled at last, they stand
    at the door,
  Watching the full-starred heavens that winter sees,
Will this thought rise on those who will meet my face no
    more,
  'He was one who had an eye for such mysteries'?

And will any say when my bell of quittance is heard in the
    gloom
  And a crossing breeze cuts a pause in its outrollings,
Till they rise again, as they were a new bell's boom,
  'He hears it not now, but used to notice such things'?

DANNIE ABSE

BOTH as a poet and as an editor Dannie Abse has always shown a healthy indifference to prevailing literary fashions. In the early 1950's, as editor of the magazine *Poetry and Poverty*, he published many young poets who today are well-known, and in his editorials adopted a generally critical attitude to the rather flat, neutral poetry then in vogue – the poetry of the so-called Movement Poets. Indeed, when in 1957 he co-edited with Howard Sergeant the anthology *Mavericks*, it was largely in order to present the work of some of the good poets who had been excluded from the recently published, Movement-dominated *New Lines* anthology. In an introductory note to *Mavericks* Dannie Abse wrote: 'Language, the Movement believes, should be straight and un-adorned. It would be all right if they were just anti-rhetorical. But the Lucky Jim attitude is – apart from anything else – fundamentally *anti-poetic*. . . . With the Movement Poets one hardly ever gets the impression that the poem has seized the poet and that a struggle has ensued between the poem and the poet, between the nameless, amorphous, Dionysian material and the conscious, law-abiding, articulating craftsman.'

By this time two books of Abse's own poems had appeared, and a third, *Tenants of the House*, was about to come out. When it did, it showed clearly that he, for one, was writing outside the Movement tradition, and what's more was prepared to take risks and look beyond his own back garden for his subject matter. The best poems in *Tenants of the House* are eloquent without being rhetorical ('Letter to the Times'), dramatic without being vulgar ('Duality', 'The Trial'), lyrical without being sweet ('Anniversary'). The achievement was summed up by the *Listener*'s poetry critic: 'Dr. Abse's admirable new book of poems shows that while the rest of us have been spending our time being smart or angry or whatever, he has quietly consolidated his position as one of the most satisfying and genuine of contemporary poets, with things to say that matter and the power to say them forcefully and originally.' The success of the volume was all the more surprising when seen within the context of Abse's earlier work, which was too inexact, too bound up with its own music and conceits (and with the music and conceits of others) to be of enduring value – though there were exceptions: the much anthologized 'Letter to Alex Comfort', for example, and the lyrical 'Epithalamion'. That Abse himself recognizes the flaws is perhaps evidenced by the fact that he included only four of the early poems in his recently published *Selected Poems*.

Abse brings to his work a wide range of experience. Born in Cardiff in 1923, he is in fact a medical doctor. Although he has lived in London more or less since qualifying, Wales in general (and Cardiff in particular) has remained important to him. This is shown clearly in poems like 'Return to Cardiff', and in his autobiographical novel *Ash On a Young Man's Sleeve*, in which he recreates vividly the Welsh-Jewish experiences of his childhood, setting them against the general troubled backcloth of the times – unemployment, the rise of Hitler and Mussolini, the Spanish Civil War, and so on. He has always had a predeliction for the dramatic, and it is not surprising that quite early on he was drawn to write for the theatre. (Out of one of the less successful poems in *Tenants of the House* – 'The Meeting' – evolved a play, *House of Cowards*, which won the Charles Henry Foyle Award.) There is also in his poetry, as well as in later plays such as *Gone*, or his recent novel *O. Jones, O. Jones*, a strong element of humour, always underpinned by an accurate observation of the strange, the ludicrous, the human.

This relationship to the real world has become an important anchor in Dannie Abse's more recent work. Whereas *Tenants of the House* displays a metaphysical approach to its various themes, his next book, *Poems, Golders Green* (1962) is deeply rooted in a specific environment – the city, or more specifically suburbia. The poems in this volume are generally more direct than hitherto, and the strong impact they have had on audiences when read aloud is hardly surprising. They are very much the poems of an outsider living in an 'in' community, and the theme of alienation, of oddity, runs through the book. One poem, 'Odd', is in many ways characteristic of the volume, contrasting the writer's inability to fit into 'nice, quiet, religious' Golders Green with his inability to fit into 'nice, dirty, irreligious' Soho. In both places he wants 'to scream' and thus 'by the neighbours' then 'by Soho friends' is considered 'odd'.

In Golders Green, of course, one's neighbours may well be Jewish, which gives this particular suburb an added dimension. In the volume there is a handful of poems touching on Jewish themes – ranging from the lyrical 'Song of a Hebrew' to the eloquent 'After the Release of Ezra Pound'. Commenting on this in the Poetry Book Society's Bulletin (the book was their Spring Choice), Abse wrote: 'Hitler made me more of a Jew than Moses'. Such 'Jewishness' as there is in the volume – and it would be wrong to dwell overlong on it – is often symbolic. Abse certainly recognizes this, for when asked in an interview whether Jewish notes entered his work, he replied: 'Sometimes, yes; and often in an obscure or arcane way. Without conscious design on my part, I find myself working, for example, on a poem about the remnant of a tree that has previously been struck by lightning. In short, a misfit of a tree rather than say, a tall, straight, beautiful elm. Or I take as subject matter a shunter – you know those slow, slave-like engines you see on railway tracks – rather than an express train. That I choose one subject rather than another, even if not consciously, seems to me to have something to do with the fact that I am a Jew living in the 20th century; and therefore someone who must be aware of the situational predicament of the Jew in a special, close way.' Certainly there is a powerful emotional charge behind these particular poems, as there is in a new poem, 'No More Mozart', included here:

> The German streets tonight
> are soaped in moonlight.
> The streets of Germany are clean
> like the hands of Lady MacBeth . . .

Throughout *Poems, Golders Green* the symbols of earlier poems recur – the mask is one favourite. There is also a sequence of lyrically haunting love poems ('Three Voices') which harks back to earlier volumes – only now the voice is sure and economical. This sureness is perhaps most striking in 'The Water Diviner', a mysterious, spiritual poem about the lack of inspiration and the self-doubt which all artists suffer – and not only artists, for the poem is about religious doubt also:

> Repeated desert, recurring drought,
> sometimes hearing water trickle,
> sometimes not, I by doubting first,
> believe; believing, doubt.

By talking about or attempting to outline a poet's themes one is of course distorting, paraphrasing the unparaphrasable. Many of the poems in Dannie Abse's most recent book, *A Small Desperation* (1968) in fact explore those areas of experience which defy articulation. Odours, distant tunes, voices behind the voices that we hear – these appeared obsessively in the earlier poems as *ideas*, never quite inhabiting them. In *A Small Desperation* they return. There are 'inviolate odours in halls', silhouettes 'running across the evening fields, knee deep in mist,' the 'darkness inside a dead man's mouth'. Disturbing images these, but concrete, and organic. And the volume *is* a deeply serious, at times grave one, which contains a number of Abse's most ambitious poems. There is in it a new, at times tragic intensity, an obsession with death, with the inanimate, with the indefinable 'nameless' things which order our existence:

> There is something else that I must do
> for some other thing is crying too
> in chaos, near, without a name.

Although the poems are patently contemporary, they avoid pat answers and glib slogans ('protesting poems, like the plaster angels/are impotent . . .'). Rather they pose questions, offer ambiguities and unusual correlations. Their range, too is impressive. There is wit and lyricism, social irony and political self-questioning. Also, there is a new element, for this is the first volume in which Abse draws on his experiences as a doctor, both thematically and as a source of imagery (as he does, too, in his latest play, *The Dogs of Pavlov*). The long last poem of the book ('The Smile Was') draws explicitly and affirmatively on the medical background, taking as its starting point the invariable, wonderful smile of a woman who has just given birth. Roland Mathias commented on this affirmative aspect of Abse's work in the *Anglo-Welsh Review*: 'He is no friend to the wry down turn, to the non-committed fragmentization so fashionable recently, to the ultimate cynicism. In his pages there is such a thing as love and, despite moments of non-communication and despair, there are also spiritual intuitions. ... The reader who is not himself unsanguine will from time to time cry "True" with the delighted recognition that one accords to something experienced

34

in life but seldom read in the work of serious modern poets.'

Such affirmations may be unusual in a world of Vietnams, yet they never seem false or merely romantic. On the contrary, as in all Dannie Abse's best work the real experience comes through compellingly – the strength of the voice, the originality of the observation and the inferences he draws from it, opening up unsuspected areas of response and potentiality in the reader and giving the poems a range and character rarely matched by the work of his contemporaries.

Dannie Abse writes:

There were few poetry books in the house. Palgrave's *Golden Treasury*, the *Oxford Book of English Verse*, and two slim Faber volumes in Leo's bookcase. These books had nothing to do with me. I was too young. Like the row of Charles Dickens and the set of Joseph Conrad, stoutly bound in navy blue with great gold lettering, they were there to be read later when I was an old teenager. My father, in his palmy days, had bought these sets along with some grey-bound, luxurious encyclopaedias from a glib travelling salesman, years before I was born.

I was a shy ten-year-old. I was interested in the fortunes of Cardiff City football club, and the Glamorgan cricket eleven. Poetry was something to do with short long short, or long short long. But Leo, seven years older than I, used to read out loud Browning's 'The Lost Leader' or 'Porphyria's Lover'. Wilfred, then nineteen, occasionally recited, 'Tears, idle tears I know not what they mean, Tears from the depth of some divine despair'. And the eldest of us, my sister Huldah, could be heard upstairs healthily singing in the echoing bathroom: 'Some day he'll come along, the man I love'. Incidentally he did, soon after.

'Tears, idle tears', or 'Some day he'll come along', were all the same to me. They were manifestations of what grown ups called 'soul'. To this day I have never heard my father recite a line from a poem. When he was gay he told jokes, when moodily sad he would take down his violin and, with eyes closed like a lover, play Kreisler's *Humoresque* until he became, for all the grey and green world of Wales, a model for Chagall. My mother exuded 'soul' any time – any time at all. She knew off by heart long stanzas and even longer stanzas of 'Hiawatha'. At the drop of an eyelid she'd be off moaning, 'O the famine and the fever! O the wasting of the famine! O the blasting of the fever! O the wailing of the children! O the anguish of the women!' And so on, until one of my elder brothers would cry: 'Put a sock in it, moth.'

Certainly I had no ambition to become a writer. I was not even particularly pleased when I won a school prize for the set essay on 'The Evils of Drink'. I didn't want to become anything. I wanted to keep on sucking mintoes for ever. 'What do you want to be when you grow up' was a question one had to endure from adults, like having cheeks pinched or being told to 'Wee wee, wash, and comb your hair'. My eldest brother, Wilfred, decided that I should be a doctor. He was going to be one. Moreover, I had two uncles who were doctors, and five cousins who were destined to wear the honourable white coat. In my family it seemed there were only two choices – either you became a doctor or went on the dole to play a marvellous game of snooker. I was neutral about the matter. Once, though, when coming home a few years later from the local flicks after seeing Paul Muni play Ehrlich in *The Magic Bullet*, I expressed some vague interest in medicine. My eyes shone with Hollywood heroics, and, before I could change my illusions, Wilfred responsibly put my name down to go to Westminster Hospital, London.

I was then attending a high school in Splott, Cardiff. Poetry was still something rather dreary like the school song: 'Green and gold, green and gold, Strong be your heart and bold, To

36

remain unsullied our great name, Adding to ancient glory, modern fame. . . .' *Ach y fee.*

But I was fortunate during those early Cardiff years for, at home, I was exposed to the adult dialogue of the 'thirties – to the dialogue between Sigmund Freud and Karl Marx, as it was interpreted and argued by my two elder brothers, by Wilfred who is now a psychiatrist and by Leo who is the M.P. for Pontypool. Leo, already, was quite a persuasive orator, and used to stand on a soap box in Llandaff Fields. I heard him once quote: 'It is given to man to live but once and he should live not to be seared by the shame of a cowardly and trivial past, but so live that dying he might say – All my life and all my strength have been given to the finest cause in the world, the enlightenment and liberation of mankind'. I was moved perhaps for the first time by words, by the order of words – not by poetry though, but by rhetoric.

Outside, in the streets of Cardiff, there were yellow, bouncing tramcars, and occasionally a hearse would pass by pulled by six coal-black horses. The newspaper headlines were about Mussolini and Abyssinia, later about Hitler and 'Last Territorial Claims'. Always J. C. Clay was taking wickets for Glamorgan and Cardiff City lost at home. BLUEBIRDS FLATTER TO DECEIVE headlined the back page, and somewhere in the middle pages of *The South Wales Echo*, Beverley Baxter irrevocably wrote about 'The Red Sea of Bolshevism'. It was colour, colour all the way, and one of my non-doctor uncles had more than a drop to drink. 'Leo will be Prime Minister one day', he said to my father, 'Wilfred's got an 'ead on 'im'. He looked at me then. 'Never mind, you've got a diabolical right foot. *Diabolical*'. And he shouted 'Up the City'.

Stimulated by my brothers' conversations and arguments I began to write essays in a little, blue exercise book. I wrote these essays in order to clarify my own attitudes. They were 'On Fascism', 'On Socialism', 'On Jazz', and so on. I showed them to Wilfred, who seriously encouraged me to write more. Wilfred was infallibly kind. But still there was no poetry in the little, blue exercise book. Just one line of Keats: 'No hungry generations tread thee down'. For that I thought was the greatest line ever written – not that I had read many lines. In this reference to a nightingale, and its inference about his own pulmonary tuberculosis, the poet had captured my youthful social conscience. After all, I knew of the miners who coughed, the T.B. that was rife in the valleys, the processions of the unemployed. That line was the embodiment of the sad, bitter soul. 'No hungry generations tread thee down. It contained my father playing *Humoresque*, my mother wailing Longfellow, quotations of Lenin, and even the lyric my sister sang in the bathroom: 'Ten cents a dance, that's what they pay me, Lord how they weigh me down' – and the old pipes in the house knocked and shook because of an air bubble.

But it was my youthful engagement with the tragedy of Spain that oddly led me to 'modern poetry'. That war seemed to me, as it did to many others much older, to be a straightforward case of white *v.* black. The *News Chronicle* used to come into the house with its bitter accounts of the fighting in Spain and its attacks on the Government's non-intervention policy. Besides, I lived in the same house as Leo and was moved by his declamatory and righteous protestations. Also, I went to a Catholic school where I was taught by Christian brothers. I was the only boy in the school who was against Franco. There is nothing like being in a minority of one, especially at fourteen years of age, to be wholly and fiercely committed to a cause – especially if that cause is a losing one. 'Do you know what the Reds would do if they came here?' said one of the brothers in his black grieving gown. 'Why, boy, they'd burn me down and the school wid me', and when my fist clenched I think he mistakenly assumed I was giving a surreptitious communist salute. 'Green and gold, green and gold, Strong be your heart and bold'.

So I find it strange to read a poem by Donald Davie, a poet and critic of my own generation, who, remembering the ninteen-thirties, writes:

The Anschluss, Guernica – all the names
At which those poets thrilled, or were afraid,
For me mean schools and schoolmasters and games;
And in the process someone is betrayed.

For me Guernica meant Cornford dead, Lorca dead, Caudwell dead, Fox dead, heroes dead, dead, dead. It meant a long fight in the back lane with the school's hooker because he saw Franco as a knight on a white horse, a protector of nuns. It meant particularly a book of poems that came out two years later. It was entitled simply *Poems for Spain* and it was edited by John Lehmann and Stephen Spender. I was moved to learn several of the poems in this anthology off by heart, including John Cornford's beautiful love poem, all the more poignant since he wrote it just before he was killed at Huesca.

And so, imitative, I too was moved to write poems. Before long I secretly sent them out to magazines like *Penguin New Writing* and *The Welsh Review*. Moreover, the rejection slips I received with little notes decorating them, 'I like many things in this', signed J.L., didn't discourage me. Not long after, war broke out and my two brothers, called up, left home. And so I was deprived of my immediate and reluctant audience.

In 1942, during my first year of medical studies at Cardiff, I resolved to show my notebook of poems to S. L. Bethell who was not only a Shakespearean scholar at the university but had also had poems published. But shy, I kept putting off my plan to ambush him. One afternoon, though, in the foyer of the university, I saw him come through the swing doors and, since I was clutching my red-hot notebook of poems in my hand, I involuntarily sidestepped towards him.

39

'Please sir', I mumbled, 'would you be kind enough to er, to er, to er . . .' He looked down at me puzzled, not knowing me from Adam. 'What?' he said. 'My poems, sir. Would you read them perhaps? I know you're busy, but—' He took the notebook off me. I wanted him, of course, to take the poems away and read them later. But he opened up the notebook there and then. I stood awkwardly by, fidgeting as students rushed in and out of the swing doors. I don't know what I expected him to say. I don't know now what I wanted him to say. But whatever he said would be of desperate importance to me. Suddenly, as he read down the page, his mouth opened slightly and he made a quiet noise. 'Pardon, sir?' I asked. The noise became louder, and his body seemed to shake. I stood there blushing and heard him distinctly: 'Ha ha ha. Ha ha ha. Ha ha ha HA HA HA HA HA. Oh ha ha, well, boy, ha ha, well well, there you are, boy'. He thrust the notebook back into my hands, and smiling cheerfully disappeared down the corridor.

I don't think Professor Bethell intended to be unkind. The poems probably merited that kind of treatment. He just had not agreed with Johnson who once said, 'The price of reading other people's poetry is praise'. But he discouraged me for a whole year in one sense: I ceased to send my poems out to the literary magazines. The following year I continued my medical studies in wartime London. Still I wrote poems. Still there was the inevitable notebook. This time the front pages consisted of notes taken during lectures on anatomy and physiology. But the back pages, as usual, were noisy with poems.

One day in 1944, after a session in the dissecting room, I saw on the notice board that the poet Edmund Blunden was to give a lecture to the literary society. So, instead of returning to my digs, I hung around till six o'clock, and then went to Blunden's lecture. I don't remember what he talked about now. I don't recall what questions I asked him afterwards. But he evidently discerned that I was interested in poetry for he invited me to have a drink with him. So clutching my note-book I, with the president and secretary and vice-president and vice-vice-secretary and vice-acting treasurer of the literary society, followed him down the Strand to a pub. He took the book away with him. I have the letter he wrote me still. It's on yolk-yellow paper and he used red ink. He was exceedingly generous, especially as I now realize that those early poems I showed him were extreme failures.

When I went home to Cardiff next I proudly read out Edmund Blunden's letter to my parents. They were baffled by his kind remarks. My father said, 'He can't be much of a critic. Besides, you should be studying medicine hard, not wasting time composing verses'. But they listened intently when I read them my newest, shining, still wet poem.

There was a puzzled silence from my parents afterwards until my mother moaned, 'O the famine and the fever, O the wasting and the famine, O the blasting of the fever!' and Dad shouted above the wailing, 'I don't care if he's Homer. He's got to earn a living'.

Reprinted from *The Listener*, March 21, 1963

ANNIVERSARY

The tree grows down from a bird.
The strong grass pulls up the earth
to a hill. Wade here, my dear
through green shallows of daisies.
I hear the voice talking that is dead
behind the voice that is talking now.
The clocks of the smoky town
strike a quiet, grating sound.
Tomorrow will be the same.
Two sit on this hill and count
two moving from the two that stayed.

What happens to a flame blown out?
What perishes? Not this view,
nor my magnified hand in yours
whatever hurt and angers done.
I breathe in air the dead breathed out.
When first you inclined your face
to mine, my sweet ally came,
with your brown eyes purely wide.
My right hand on your left breast
I said, I have little to tell my dear.
For the pure bird, a pure cage.

Oh the silence that you lost
blind in the pandemonium
of the kiss and ruined was.
My dear, my dear, what perishes?
I hear this voice in a voice to come.

RETURN TO CARDIFF

'Hometown'; well, most admit an affection for a city:
grey, tangled streets I cycled on to school, my first cigarette
in the back lane, and fool, my first botched love affair.
First everything. Faded torments; self-indulgent pity.

The journey to Cardiff seemèd less a return than a raid
on mislaid identities. Of course the whole locus smaller:
the mile-wide Taff now a stream, the castle not as in some black
gothic dream, but a decent sprawl, a joker's toy façade.

Unfocused voices in the wind, associations, clues,
odds and ends, fringes caught, as when, after the doctor quit,
a door opened and I glimpsed the white, enormous face
of my grandfather, suddenly aghast with certain news.

Unable to define anything I can hardly speak,
and still I love the place for what I wanted it to be
as much as for what it unashamedly is
now for me, a city of strangers, alien and bleak.

Unable to communicate I'm easily betrayed,
uneasily diverted by mere sense reflections
like those anchored waterscapes that wander, alter, in the Taff,
hour by hour, as light slants down a different shade.

Illusory, too, that lost, dark playground after rain,
the noise of trams, gunshots in what they once called Tiger Bay.
Only real this smell of ripe, damp earth when the sun comes out,
a mixture of pungencies, half exquisite and half plain.

No sooner than I'd arrived the other Cardiff had gone,
smoke in the memory, these but tinned resemblances,
where the boy I was not and the man I am not
met, hesitated, left double footsteps, then walked on.

CHALK

Chalk, calcium carbonate, should mean school –
a small, neutral stick neither cool nor hot,
its smell should evoke wooden desks slamming
when, squeaking over blackboards, it could not
decently teach us more than one plus one.

Now, no less pedagogic in ruder districts,
on iron railway bridges, where urchins fight,
an urgent scrawl names our failure – BAN THE BOMB,
or more peculiarly, KEEP BRITAIN WHITE.
Chalk, it seems, has some bleeding purposes.

In the night, secretly, they must have come,
strict, clenched men in the street, anonymous,
past closed shops and the sound of running feet
till upstairs, next morning, vacant in a bus,
we observe a once blank wall assaulted.

There's not enough chalk in the wronged world
to spell out one plus one, the perfect lies.
HANDS OFF GUATEMALA – though slogans change,
never the chalk scraping on the pitched noise
of a nerve in violence or in longing.

PATHOLOGY OF COLOURS

I know the colour rose, and it is lovely,
but not when it ripens in a tumour;
and healing greens, leaves and grass, so springlike,
in limbs that fester are not springlike.

I have seen red-blue tinged with hirsute mauve
in the plum-skin face of a suicide.
I have seen white, china white almost, stare
from behind the smashed windscreen of a car.

And the criminal, multi-coloured flash
of an H-bomb is no more beautiful
than an autopsy when the belly's opened –
to show cathedral windows never opened.

So in the simple blessing of a rainbow,
in the bevelled edge of a sunlit mirror,
I have seen, visible, Death's artifact
like a soldier's ribbon on a tunic tacked.

THE WATER DIVINER

Late, I have come to a parched land
doubting my gift, if gift I have,
the inspiration of water
spilt, swallowed in the sand.

To hear once more water trickle,
to stand in a stretch of silence
the divine pen twisting in the hand:
sign of depths alluvial.

Water owns no permanent shape,
brags, is most itself in chaos;
now, under the shadow of the idol,
dry mouth and dry landscape.

No rain falls with a refreshing sound
to settle tubular in a well,
elliptical in a bowl. No grape
lusciously moulds it round.

Clouds have no constant resemblance
to anything, blown by a hot wind,
flying mirages; the blue background,
light constructions of chance.

To hold back chaos I transformed
amorphous mass: clay, fire, or cloud,
so that the agèd gods might dance
and golden structures form.

I should have built, plain brick on brick,
a water tower. The sun flies on
arid wastes, barren hells too warm,
and me with a hazel stick!

Rivulets vanished in the dust
long ago, great compositions
vaporized, salt on the tongue so thick
that drinking, still I thirst.

Repeated desert, recurring drought,
sometimes hearing water trickle,
sometimes not, I, by doubting first,
believe; believing, doubt.

MISS BOOK WORLD

We, the judges, a literary lot,
peep-Tom legitimately at these beauties,
give marks for legs and breasts, make remarks
low or pompous like most celebrities.
Not that we are, but they imagine us so
who parade blatantly as camera-lights flash
crazily for a glossy page and cash.

Perhaps some girls entered for a giggle,
but all walk slave-like in this ritual fuss
of unfunny compère, funny applause,
spotlit dream-girls displayed, a harem for us,
not that they are, but we imagine them so,
with Miss Book World herself just barely flawed,
almost perfect woman, almost perfect fraud.

The illusion over, half the contestants
still fancy themselves in their knock-out pose,
while we literati return to the real
world of fancy, great poetry and prose,
not that it is, but we imagine it so,
great vacant visions in which we delight,
as if we see the stars not only at night.

AS I WAS SAYING

Yes, madam, as a poet I *do* take myself seriously,
and, since I have a young, questioning family, I suppose
I should know something about English wild flowers:
the shape of their leaves, when this and that one grows,
how old mythologies attribute strange powers
to this or that one. Urban, I should mug up anew
the pleasant names: Butterbur, Ling, and Lady's Smock,
Jack-by-the-Hedge, Cuckoo-Pint, and Feverfew,
even the Stinking Hellebore – all in that W. H. Smith book
I could bring home for myself (inscribed to my daughter)
to swot, to know which is this and which that one,
what honours the high cornfield, what the low water,
under the slow-pacing clouds and occasional sun
of England.
    But no! Done for in the ignorant suburb,
I'll drink Scotch, neurotically stare through glass
at the rainy lawn, at green stuff, nameless birds,
and let my daughter, madam, go to nature class.
I'll not compete with those nature poets you advance,
some in country dialect, and some in dialogue
with the country – few as calm as their words:
Wordsworth, Barnes, sad John Clare who ate grass.

INTERVIEW WITH A SPIRIT HEALER

Smiling, he says no man should fear the tomb
for where we fade the grass is greener.
Listen! Someone coughs in his waiting room;
then, from upstairs, the suburban howl of
the made ghost in a vacuum cleaner.

With nude emotion, he names the miracles
as hip fans would football matches.
His voice catches on the incurably cured
whose letters, testimonials, conclude,
'. . . though the doctors gave me up as hopeless'.

His tragic venue, those frayed English spas:
Cheltenham, Leamington, Tunbridge, Bath,
where depressed male Tories, on their sticks,
guzzle in chromium and maroon hotel bars
which seem more empty when people whisper.

He murmurs, 'Love', which could be disturbing,
also 'Spirit guides'. Look, his upraised hand
show neither its knuckles nor its palm,
and, like a candle in daytime burning,
seems but a sign ethereal as a psalm.

Goodbye! His spirituality is too inbred,
too indelible like a watermark;
and I, gross sceptic hired by a paper,
prefer my dead to be in the dark.
Goodbye. His eyes, Mary's blue, stare at vapour.

Let him, in faith, stare on. I loathe his trade,
the disease and the sanctimonious lie

that cannot cure the disease. My need,
being healthy, is not faith; but to curse the day
I became mortal the night my father died.

HUNT THE THIMBLE

Hush now. You cannot describe it.

Is it like heavy rain falling,
and lights going on, across the fields,
in the new housing estate?

Cold, cold. Too domestic, too
temperate, too devoid of history.

Is it like a dark windowed street at night,
the houses uncurtained, the street deserted?

Colder. You are getting colder,
and too romantic, too dream-like.
You cannot describe it.

The brooding darkness then,
that breeds inside a cathedral
of a provincial town in Spain?

In Spain, also, but not Spanish.
In England, if you like, but not English.
It remains, even when obscure, perpetually.
Aged, but ageless, you cannot describe it.
No, you are cold, altogether too cold.

Aha – the blue sky over Ampourias,
the blue sky over Lancashire for that matter . . .

You cannot describe it.

. . . obscured by clouds?
I must know what you mean.

Hush, hush.

Like those old men in hospital dying,
who, unaware strangers stand around their bed,
stare obscurely, for a long moment,
at one of their own hands raised –
which perhaps is bigger than the moon again –
and then, drowsy, wandering, shout out, 'Mama'.

Is it like that? Or hours after that even:
the darkness inside a dead man's mouth?

No, no, I have told you:
you are cold, and you cannot describe it.

A NEW DIARY

This clerk-work, this first January chore
of who's in, who's out. A list to think about
when absences seem to shout, Scandal! Outrage!
So turning to the blank, prefatory page
I transfer most of the names and phone tags
from last year's diary. True, Meadway, Speedwell,
Mountview, are computer-changed into numbers,
and already their pretty names begin to fade
like Morwenna, Julie, Don't-Forget-Me-Kate,
grassy summer girls I once swore love to.
These, whispering others and time will date.

Cancelled, too, a couple someone else betrayed,
one man dying, another mind in rags.
And remembering them my clerk-work flags,
bitterly flags, for all lose, no-one wins,
those in, those out, *this* at the heart of things.
So I stop, ask: whom should I commemorate,
and who, perhaps, is crossing out my name
now from some future diary? Oh my God,
Morwenna, Julie, don't forget me, Kate.

NO MORE MOZART

High to the right a hill of trees,
a fuselage of branches
reflects German moonlight
like dull armour.
Sieg heil!

Higher still, one moon migrates deathwards,
a white temper between clouds.
To the left, the other slides
undulating on the black,
oiled, rippling reservoir.

Can't sleep for Mozart,
and on the winter glass
a shilling's worth of glitter.

The German streets tonight
are soaped in moonlight.
The streets of Germany are clean
like the hands of Lady Macbeth.

Back in bed the eyes close, do not sleep.
Achtung! Achtung!
Someone is breathing nearby,
someone not accounted for,
like a ghost on barbed wire,
someone dumb, it seems.
The gasmask goggles on a skull.

Now, of course, no more Mozart.
With eyes closed still
the body touches itself, takes stock.

Above the hands the thin wrists
attached to them; and on the wrists
the lampshade material.
Also the little hairs that can be pulled.

The eyes open:
the German earth is made of helmets;
the wind seeps through a deep
frost hole that is somewhere else
carrying the far Jew-sounds of railway trucks.

Nothing is annulled:
the blood vow, the undecorated cry,
someone robbed of his name,
a grenade, a decapitation,
and the wind-pipe whistling.
Then silence again.

Afterwards:
the needle rests on a record
with nothing on that record turning,
neither sound nor silence,
nothing at all,
for it is sleep at last.

There, the fugitive body has arrived
at the stink of nothing.
And twelve million eyes
in six million heads
stare in the same direction.

Outside, the electrician works
inside his cloud, silently,
and the reservoir darkens.

Germany 1970

FORGOTTEN

That old country I once said I'd visit
when older. Can no-one tell me its name?
Odd, to have forgotten what it is called.
I would recognize the name if I heard it.
So many times I have searched the atlas
with a prowling convex lens – to no avail.

I know the geography of the great world
has changed: the war, the peace, the deletions
of places – red pieces gone forever,
and names of countries altered forever:
Gold Coast Ghana, Persia become Iran,
Siam Thailand, and hell now Vietnam.

People deleted. Must I sleep to reach it,
to find the back door opening to a field,
a barking of dogs, and a path that leads back?
One night in pain, the dead middle of night,
will I awake again, know who I am,
the man from somewhere else, and the place's name?

VERNON SCANNELL

PARTLY through the many readings and broadcasts he has given over the past few years, Vernon Scannell has won himself a faithful following of discerning readers. Nevertheless, his last volume at any rate received less than its critical due in the British press, and in America his work remains unpublished in book form. Scannell's life has been a varied and colourful one, as his recent autobiography *The Tiger and the Rose* shows, and his poetry often mirrors its various facets. Born in 1922, he served during the Second World War with the Gordon Highlanders in North Africa and Normandy, spent a year at Leeds University, has boxed professionally, written six books of poems, five novels, and numerous features and plays for radio.

Although imagination and craftsmanship may have brought about their necessary transformations and elaborations, the core of Scannell's poems remains deeply bedded in direct experience and observation: however he may disguise the experience, however he may project it, the feeling that the poem has been lived is always there. Scannell himself has admired this approach in others: 'I don't think poets generally have been preoccupied with the great abstractions and eternal verities. I think they have always, the best of them, anyway, had their preoccupations rooted in lived experience. I think this must be so. ... I think the poet should aim at absolute honesty, total fidelity to the experience, whatever it may be, which has started the poem off, and, calling upon all his resources of technique, imagination, intelligence, vocabulary and memory he should build a structure of words which, working upon both the conscious and unconscious instruments of perception in his reader, will thrill him in a way no other art form can do.'

The emphasis he places on intelligence, imagination and technique is not fortuitous. If one examines his *Selected Poems* (Allison & Busby, 1971), the variety of the verse forms, the direct power of the language, the sharpness and accuracy of observation, are precisely the qualities which strike one most forcefully – though one should point also to the exceptional narrative skill, for like Thomas Hardy (a poet Scannell admires greatly) he brings to his poetry all the attributes of a born story teller. Many of the poems may indeed be loosely described as concentrated or heightened short stories. Often the poems focus on an incident or character, sometimes working on an intense dramatic level, sometimes on a lighter more ironic one, though the apparently lighter poems often have a kick in their tail, relying on some closely observed human absurdity to throw the character-study into reverse, removing the ready smile from the reader's lips. In 'Taken in Adultery' this technique may be seen at work. In this case, however, the tone and approach are ominous from the word 'go', the precise and witty observation of place (a public bar) and of people (a middle-aged couple having an affair) forcing the reader to identify with the situation, as one senses the poet has done:

> When they are silent each seems listening;
> There must be many voices in the air:
> Reproaches, accusations, suffering
> That no amount of passion keeps elsewhere.
> Imperatives that brought them to this room,
> Stiff from the car's back seat, lose urgency;
> They start to wonder who's betraying whom,
> How it will end, and how did it begin –

The woman taken in adultery
And the man who feels he, too, was taken in.

Those lovers are but two of the many characters who are
given voice and life in Vernon Scannell's poetry. Colonels,
batmen, boxers, travelling salesmen, disc jockeys and a host of
other memorables are scattered through the pages of his
various books. Yet his poems seem to me most moving when
the eye turns inwards, as it often does, the self-awareness and
unaffected honesty forcing one to respond at the deepest level.
'My Father's Face', 'Death in the Lounge Bar', and 'The Men
Who Wear My Clothes' are all poems which command this
kind of response, not simply because they are honest but
because the honesty has been mated to a critical intelligence
which has ordered the experience in a firm way:

> The men who wear my clothes walked past my bed
> And all of them looked tired and rather old;
> I felt a chip of ice melt in my blood.
> Naked I lay last night and very cold.

Essentially Scannell is a traditionalist in that scarcely any of
his poems depart from established forms, though this is not to
say that the verse is any way mechanical or irrelevant to its
content. In fact, he takes traditional metres and rhyme-
patterns and adapts them so that they can carry, without
strain, an easy colloquial tone which is able to rise to moments
of dramatic and lyrical intensity. He has said that he agrees
with Robert Frost's remark that free verse is 'like playing
tennis without a net', and he himself has worked with apparent
ease in a wide variety of forms, from sonnet-sequences and the
regular stanzas of 'My Father's Face' – a poem which fulfils
Yeats' ideal requirement that there should be a perfect coincidence between the sense unit and the stanza – to the sprung
rhythms of 'An Old Lament Renewed', and the complex

patterns of rhyme and half-rhyme and the metrical shiftings evident in 'End of a Season'.

If I have so far avoided any mention of war, it is largely because Scannell has become associated with the Second World War to such an extent that much of his other subject matter has been overlooked or only nodded to in passing. Undoubtedly the war was for him a 'climactic experience'. Often he weaves the imagery and vocabulary of war into poems whose theme is not war (in the way he draws on boxing imagery), not for ornamentation but out of some organic need. The importance of the war experience may be gauged from the fact that the title-poems of his last two individual collections were war poems – *Walking Wounded* (1965) and *Epithets of War* (1969). 'Epithets of War' (a poem in five parts, too long to include here) is a moving and eloquent elegy for the two world wars, to those who fought in them, and to a particular era and set of values. Though the poem's narrative line is gripping in itself, it is the compression and eye for detail which give its embattled landscapes their haunting authenticity. Mr. Scannell has an unfair advantage over many of today's 'war poets' in that he actually fought in one. And it shows – in the brickwork, certainly, but also in the compassion and sureness of touch, in the tang of it all. The sequence is a considerable achievement, skilfully structured and memorable for that vivid company of characters who parade through its final coda like ghosts on a dance floor – Corporal Mick McGuire, back from Alamein, Les King, 'who crooned like Bing', and the many others,

> Whose faces, though familiar, fade and blur.
> The bugle publishes another cry.
> Two more commands explode; butts and boots
> Crash and ring; another echoing shout
> And, by the left, they start to march away.
> The steady tramping dims into a mist.

The stone ground stretches in its vacancy;
One final flick of flag, the mist comes down,
And silence stuns with its enormous weight,
And there is nothing left to do but sleep.

Many of the same qualities are apparent too in 'Walking Wounded', 'a solemn requiem' (to quote the *Sunday Times* critic) 'with the dignity of Owen and Sassoon'. The poem is drawn from life, as Scannell explained in an interview: 'This was an actual incident in Normandy, seeing those men in the early morning coming back from an attack, and it had been lying there for nearly twenty years before I found my way to writing it. I spent an enormous amount of time on that poem and did about ten different versions before I got it out.' The same, one imagines, must be true of 'An Old Lament Renewed', a poem which touches on war, if only within the more general context of human mortality. It too has clearly grown out of deeply felt, long savoured experience. Its title is an echo of William Dunbar's great elegaic poem, *Lament for the Makers*, and in this poem Scannell discards any attempt to create a persona. Thus the poem is more directly personal than usual, the 'I' more noticeable and becoming more dominant as the theme develops:

And in a French orchard lies whatever is left
   Of my friend, Gordon Rennie, whose courage would
      toughen
The muscle of resolution; he laughed
   At death's serious face, but once too often.

On summer evenings when the religious sun stains
   The gloom in the bar and the glasses surrender demurely
I think of Donovan whose surrender was unconditional,
   That great thirst swallowed entirely.

63

And often some small thing will summon the memory
    Of my small son, Benjamin. A smile is his sweet ghost.
But behind, in the dark, the white twigs of his bones
    Form a pattern of guilt and waste.

I find the poem affecting and genuinely moving. The compassion and tenderness displayed are not commonly found in
contemporary poetry, and when they are, they are rarely
handled so surely. This same tenderness is seen again, on a
smaller, more domestic canvas in 'Growing Pains' and in a
recent poem, 'Battlefields'. Such poems counterbalance and
add another dimension to the humour, epigrammatic wit and
irony for which Vernon Scannell has been justly noted.

Vernon Scannell writes:

The poetry that you enjoy reading and perhaps trying to
write depends on the kind of person you are. If this remark
seems obvious beyond the point of banality we might reflect
that most critics and teachers of English Literature, at whatever level, work on the contrary assumption that the reader,
whatever his temperamental predispositions, needs, prejudices,
environment, intellect, and education, is – or should be – equally
responsive to all kinds of poetry, to Spenser as to Blake for
instance, or to Pope as to Hopkins. Of course it is a fact that
the wider the reader's taste the luckier he is, but most of us
have a natural bias towards certain kinds of poetry just as we
have a taste for certain kinds of food and drink (though our
preferences may change with changing circumstances) and
these predilections are determined by social, biological and
psychological factors over which we have no control.

Outside poetry my interest and sympathy are gained by
whatever breathes, moves, suffers and delights, by whatever
lives, and I am much less concerned with inanimate things.

Technological marvels, abstract sculpture and painting, objects – natural or manufactured – however beautiful they may be to others, hold comparatively little appeal for me. The nearest I come to taking an interest in anything scientific is some desultory reading in psychology and anthropology both of which, of course, are directly concerned with human life. Not surprisingly, the kind of poetry that grips me is that which is firmly rooted in the living soil of recognizable human experience. I am well aware that this is a limiting and probably naïve stance and, further, I am frequently shaken by finding myself moved and excited by poetry I would not have expected to appeal to me – by Wallace Stevens, for example, who has said, 'Life is not people and scene but thought and feeling' – but, in the main, it is the poetry of passion, of love, fear, hate, longing, wit, tenderness, violence and despair, the poetry which springs from the ground of common experience and contains the ambiguities and ironies that life itself contains, that offers me most nourishment, and writing of this kind is, of course, in the mainstream of English poetry from Chaucer, through the great Elizabethans and Jacobeans, on to Cowper, Crabbe, Wordsworth and Browning, to Hardy, Edward Thomas and W. H. Auden, the finest poet now writing in English, whatever claims are put forward from either side of the Atlantic.

Very broadly speaking, there are three main kinds of poetry being written today in England: there is the pop and public poetry of protest, written for the voice rather than the page (on which, if it gets there, it generally looks pretty thin), work which is more closely related either to the entertainment world or the political soapbox rather than to any respectable literary ancestry; there is the mainstream, earth-rooted poetry I have mentioned and, finally, the neo-academic, attenuated and bloodless writing largely inspired by the American Black Mountain poets. These categories overlap a good deal, but in their extreme forms I have little time for the first and third, the first because, far from using language poetically (that is with maximum precision) it slops out the stock epithets, phrases and images of the ad-man and pop lyricist and sets out to elicit the same stock responses; the third because it derives from what could be called the autotelic heresy, the view that maintains that it is impertinent to ask what a poem is *about*: a poem is not about anything, it simply exists, an autonomous verbal structure referring to nothing beyond itself. The trouble with this theory is that it does contain particles of truth, but to ask what a poem is about seems to me a perfectly valid question though I concede that the answer, unless it be a reading of the poem, can be no more than partial and most certainly cannot replace the poem itself.

Despite Eliot's reference to meaning in a poem as a 'bit of nice meat for the house dog' I believe that the content or meaning of the poem is vitally important, a view that would not have been questioned in any other age but the present, and for me the meaning should relate to the common bond of shared human experience. Poems about poetry, about others arts or about themselves generally leave me pretty cold. I am suspicious of abstraction in poetry: one may start with ideas but if they are to come alive, if the poem is to be properly achieved, they must be embodied, translated into things. To put it very simply: a poem which has 'alienation' for its theme should not contain the word *alienation* nor, ideally, any abstract noun at all. The poet should find a situation, a confluence of events, things, images, that presents his subject as a tenable structure. If poetry has any identifiably useful function it is this: poems allow the reader to enter modes of consciousness that would otherwise be entirely closed and incomprehensible. A simple example: I am not moved by the theologians' abstract speculations on the nature of God's love or on damnation as the sense of separation from God. These are rhetorical phrases which make little impact on my imagination. But, when I read Herbert's poems, charged with the naked feeling of the love of God, or Hopkins's terrible sonnets of religious despair, I am permitted direct access to the experiences from which the poems came. I – sceptical and, at least superficially, irreligious – suddenly know just what it feels like to be a convinced Christian in moments both of joyous affirmation and despairing anguish and I believe that my capacity for sympathy and tolerance is thereby enlarged. If any poem of mine has given any reader an inkling of what it is like to be other than himself, I would be well pleased. If not I am still content because, in the writing of a poem, whatever the merit of the completed work, I have been able to use language as an exploratory instrument for delving into the mysteries of my own experience and occasionally I have discovered that I am other than I believed myself to be and this – as Simone Weill has said – is the beginning of forgiveness.

THE TELEPHONE NUMBER

Searching for a lost address I find,
Among dead papers in a dusty drawer,
A diary which has lain there quite ten years,
And soon forget what I am looking for,
Intrigued by cryptic entries in a hand
Resembling mine but noticeably more
Vigorous than my present quavering scrawl.
Appointments – kept or not, I don't remember –
With people now grown narrow, fat or bald;
A list of books that somehow I have never
Found the time to read, nor ever shall,
Remind me that my world is growing cold.
And then I find a scribbled code and number,
The urgent words: 'Must not forget to call.'
But now, of course, I have no recollection
Of telephoning anyone at all.

The questions whisper: Did I dial that number
And, if I did, what kind of voice replied?
Questions that will never find an answer
Unless – the thought is serpentine – I tried
To telephone again, as years ago
I did, or meant to do. What would I find
If now I lifted this mechanic slave
Black to my ear and spun the dial – so ...?
Inhuman, impolite, the double burp
Erupts, insulting hope. The long dark sleeve
Of silence stretches out. No stranger's voice
Slips in, suspicious, cold; no manic speech
Telling what I do not wish to know
Nor throaty message creamed with sensual greed –
Nothing of these. And when again I try,
Relief is tearful when there's no reply.

MY FATHER'S FACE

Each morning, when I shave, I see his face,
Or something like a sketch of it gone wrong;
The artist caught, it seems, more than a trace
Of that uneasy boldness and the strong
Fear behind the stare which tried to shout
How tough its owner was, inviting doubt.

And though this face is altogether more
Loosely put together, and indeed
A lot less handsome, weaker in the jaw
And softer in the mouth, I feel no need
To have it reassembled, made a better
Copy of the face of its begetter.

I do not mind because my mouth is not
That lipless hyphen, military, stern;
He had the face that faces blade and shot
In schoolboys' tales, and even schoolboys learn
To laugh at it. But they've not heard it speak
Those bayonet words that guard the cruel and weak.

For weakness was his one consistency;
And when I scrape the soapy fluff away
I see that he bequeathed this gift to me
Along with various debts I cannot pay.
But he gave, too, this mirror-misting breath
Whose mercy dims the looking-glass of death;

For which kind accident I thank him now
And, though I cannot love him, feel a sort
Of salty tenderness, remembering how
The prude and lecher in him moiled and fought
Their roughhouse in the dark ring of his pride
And killed each other when his body died.

This morning, as I shave, I find I can
Forgive the blows, the meanness and the lust,
The ricochetting arsenal of a man
Who groaned groin-deep in hope's ironic dust;
But these eyes in the glass regard the living
Features with distaste, quite unforgiving.

THE MEN WHO WEAR MY CLOTHES

Sleepless I lay last night and watched the slow
    Procession of the men who wear my clothes:
First, the grey man with bloodshot eyes and sly
    Gestures miming what he loves and loathes.

Next came the cheery knocker-back of pints,
    The beery joker, never far from tears
Whose loud and public vanity acquaints
    The careful watcher with his private fears.

And then I saw the neat-mouthed gentle man
    Defer politely, listen to the lies,
Smile at the tedious talk and gaze upon
    The little mirrors in the speaker's eyes.

The men who wear my clothes walked past my bed
    And all of them looked tired and rather old;
I felt a chip of ice melt in my blood.
    Naked I lay last night and very cold.

I'M COVERED NOW

'What would happen to your lady wife
And little ones – you've four I think you said –
Little ones I mean, not wives, ha-ha –
What would happen to them if . . .' And here
He cleared his throat of any reticence.
'. . . if something happened to you? We've got to face
These things, must be realistic, don't you think?
Now, we have various schemes to give you cover
And, taking in account your age and means,
This policy would seem to be the one . . .'

The words uncoiled effortless but urgent,
Assured, yet coming just a bit too fast,
A little breathless, despite the ease of manner,
An athlete drawing near the tape's last gasp
Yet trying hard to seem still vigorous there.
But no, this metaphor has too much muscle;
His was an indoor art and every phrase
Was handled with a trained seducer's care.
I took the words to heart, or, if not heart,
Some region underneath intelligence,
The area where the hot romantic aria
And certain kinds of poetry are received.
And this Giovanni of the fast buck knew
My humming brain was pleasurably numb;
My limbs were weakening; he would soon achieve
The now sequestered ends for which he'd come.

At last I nodded, glazed, and said I'd sign,
But he showed little proper satisfaction.
He sighed and sounded almost disappointed,
And I remembered hearing someone say
No Juan really likes an easy lay.

But I'll say this: he covered up quite quickly
And seemed almost as ardent as before
When he pressed my hand and said that he was happy
And hoped that I was, too.

                         And then the door
Was closed behind him as our deal was closed.
If something happened I was covered now.
Odd that I felt so chilly, so exposed.

A mammoth morning moved grey flanks and groaned.
In the rusty hedges pale rags of mist hung;
The gruel of mud and leaves in the mauled lane
Smelled sweet, like blood. Birds had died or flown,
Their green and silent attics sprouting now
With branches of leafed steel, hiding round eyes
And ripe grenades ready to drop and burst.
In the ditch at the cross-roads the fallen rider lay
Hugging his dead machine and did not stir
At crunch of mortar, tantrum of a Bren
Answering a Spandau's manic jabber.
Then into sight the ambulances came,
Stumbling and churning past the broken farm,
The amputated sign-post and smashed trees,
Slow wagonloads of bandaged cries, square trucks
That rolled on ominous wheels, vehicles
Made mythopoeic by their mortal freight
And crimson crosses on the dirty white.
This grave procession passed, though, for a while,
The grinding of their engines could be heard,
A dark noise on the pallor of the morning,
Dark as dried blood; and then it faded, died.
The road was empty, but it seemed to wait –
Like a stage which knows the cast is in the wings –
Wait for a different traffic to appear.
The mist still hung in snags from dripping thorns;
Absent-minded guns still sighed and thumped.
And then they came, the walking wounded,
Straggling the road like convicts loosely chained,
Dragging at ankles exhaustion and despair.
Their heads were weighted down by last night's lead,
And eyes still drank the dark. They trailed the night
Along the morning road. Some limped on sticks;

Others wore rough dressings, splints and slings;
A few had turbanned heads, the dirty cloth
Brown-badged with blood. A humble brotherhood,
Not one was suffering from a lethal hurt,
They were not magnified by noble wounds,
There was no splendour in that company.
And yet, remembering after eighteen years,
In the heart's throat a sour sadness stirs;
Imagination pauses and returns
To see them walking still, but multiplied
In thousands now. And when heroic corpses
Turn slowly in their decorated sleep
And every ambulance has disappeared
The walking wounded still trudge down that lane,
And when recalled they must bear arms again.

TAKEN IN ADULTERY

Shadowed by shades and spied upon by glass
Their search for privacy conducts them here,
With an irony that neither notices,
To a public house; the wrong time of the year
For outdoor games; where, over gin and tonic,
Best bitter and potato crisps, they talk
Without much zest, almost laconic,
Flipping an occasional remark.
Would you guess that they were lovers, this dull pair?
The answer, I suppose, is yes, you would.
Despite her spectacles and faded hair
And his worn look of being someone's Dad
You know that they are having an affair
And neither finds it doing them much good.
Presumably, in one another's eyes,
They must look different from what we see,
Desirable in someway, otherwise
They'd hardly choose to come here, furtively,
And mutter their bleak needs above the mess
Of fag-ends, crumpled cellophane and crumbs,
Their love-feast's litter. Though they might profess
To find great joy together, all that comes
Across to us is tiredness, melancholy.
When they are silent each seems listening;
There must be many voices in the air:
Reproaches, accusations, suffering
That no amount of passion keeps elsewhere.
Imperatives that brought them to this room,
Stiff from the car's back seat, lose urgency;
They start to wonder who's betraying whom,
How it will end, and how did it begin –
The woman taken in adultery
And the man who feels he, too, was taken in.

DEATH IN THE LOUNGE BAR

The bar he went inside was not
A place he often visited;
He welcomed anonymity;
No one to switch inquisitive
Receivers on, no one could see,
Or wanted to, exactly what
He was, or had been, or would be;
A quiet brown place, a place to drink
And let thought simmer like good stock,
No mirrors to distract, no fat
And calculating face of clock,
A good calm place to sip and think.
If anybody noticed that
He was even there they'd see
A fairly tall and slender man,
Fair-haired, blue-eyed, and handsome in
A manner strictly masculine.
They would not know, or want to know,
More than what they saw of him,
Nor would they wish to bug the bone
Walls of skull and listen in
To whatever whisperings
Pittered quietly in that dark:
An excellent place to sip your gin.
Then – sting of interruption! voice
Pierced the private walls and shook
His thoughtful calm with delicate shock.
A waiter, with white napkin face
And shining toe-cap hair, excused
The oiled intrusion, asking if
His name was what indeed it was.
In that case he was wanted on
The telephone the customers used,

The one next to the Gents. He went.
Inside the secretive warm box
He heard his wife's voice, strangled by
Distance, darkness, coils of wire,
But unmistakably her voice,
Asking why he was so late,
Why did he humiliate
Her in every way he could,
Make her life so hard to face?
She'd telephoned most bars in town
Before she'd finally tracked him down.
He said that he'd been working late
And slipped in for a quick one on
His weary journey home. He'd come
Back at once. Right now. Toot sweet.
No, not another drop. Not one.
Back in the bar, he drank his gin
And ordered just one more, the last.
And just as well: his peace had gone;
The place no longer welcomed him.
He saw the waiter moving past,
That pale ambassador of gloom,
And called him over, asked him how
He had known which customer
To summon to the telephone.
The waiter said, 'Your wife described
You, sir. I knew you instantly.'
'And how did she describe me, then,
That I'm so easily recognized?'
'She said: grey suit, cream shirt, blue tie,
That you were fairly tall, red-faced,
Stout, middle-aged, and going bald.'
Disbelief cried once and sat
Bolt upright, then it fell back dead.
'Stout, middle-aged, and going bald.'

The slender ghost with golden hair
Watched him go into the cold
Dark outside, heard his slow tread
Fade towards wife, armchair, and bed.

AN OLD LAMENT RENEWED

The soil is savoury with their bones' lost marrow;
  Down among dark roots their polished knuckles lie,
And no one could tell one peeled head from another;
  Earth packs each crater that once gleamed with eye.

Colonel and batman, emperor and assassin,
  Democratised by silence and corruption,
Defy identification with identical grin:
  The joke is long, will brook no interruption.

At night the imagination walks like a ghoul
  Among the stone lozenges and counterpanes of turf
Tumescent under cypresses; the long, rueful call
  Of the owl soars high and then wheels back to earth.

And brooding over the enormous dormitory
  The mind grows shrill at those nothings in lead rooms
Who were beautiful once or dull and ordinary,
  But loved, all loved, all called to sheltering arms.

Many I grieve with a grave, deep love
  Who are deep in the grave, whose faces I never saw:
Poets who died of alcohol, bullets, or birthdays
  Doss in the damp house, forbidden now to snore.

And in a French orchard lies whatever is left
  Of my friend, Gordon Rennie, whose courage would
    toughen
The muscle of resolution; he laughed
  At death's serious face, but once too often.

On summer evenings when the religious sun stains
  The gloom in the bar and the glasses surrender demurely

I think of Donovan whose surrender was unconditional,
   That great thirst swallowed entirely.

And often some small thing will summon the memory
   Of my small son, Benjamin. A smile is his sweet ghost.
But behind, in the dark, the white twigs of his bones
   Form a pattern of guilt and waste.

I am in mourning for the dull, the heroic and the mad;
   In the haunted nursery the child lies dead.
I mourn the hangman and his bulging complement;
   I mourn the cadaver in the egg.

The one-eyed rider aims, shoots death into the womb;
   Blood on the sheet of snow, the maiden dead.
The dagger has a double blade and meaning,
   So has the double bed.

Imagination swaggers in the sensual sun
   But night will find it at the usual mossy gate;
The whisper from the mouldering darkness comes:
   'I am the one you love and fear and hate.'

I know my grieving is made thick by terror;
   The bones of those I loved aren't fleshed by sorrow.
I mourn the deaths I've died and go on dying;
   I fear the long, implacable tomorrow.

GROWING PAIN

The boy was barely five years old.
We sent him to the little school
And left him there to learn the names
Of flowers in jam jars on the sill
And learn to do as he was told.
He seemed quite happy there until
Three weeks afterwards, at night,
The darkness whimpered in his room.
I went upstairs, switched on his light,
And found him wide awake, distraught,
Sheets mangled and his eiderdown
Untidy carpet on the floor.
I said, 'Why can't you sleep? A pain?'
He snuffled, gave a little moan,
And then he spoke a single word:
'Jessica.' The sound was blurred.
'Jessica? What do you mean?'
'A girl at school called Jessica,
She hurts –' he touched himself between
The heart and stomach '– she has been
Aching here and I can see her.'
Nothing I had read or heard
Instructed me in what to do.
I covered him and stroked his head.
'The pain will go, in time,' I said.

BATTLEFIELDS

Tonight in the pub I talked with Ernie Jones
Who served with the Somersets in Normandy,
And we remembered how our fathers told
The sad and muddy legends of their war,
And how, as youngsters, we would grin and say:
'The old man's on his favourite topic now;
He never tires of telling us the tale.'
We are the old men now, our turn has come.
The names have changed: Tobruk and Alamein,
Arnhem, the Falaise Gap and Caen Canal
Displace the Dardanelles, Gallipoli,
Vimy Ridge, The Somme; but little else.
Our children do not want to hear about
The days when we were young and, sometimes, brave.
And who can blame them? Certainly not us.
We drank a last half-pint and said goodnight.
And now, at home, the family is in bed,
The kitchen table littered with crashed 'planes;
A tank is tilted on its side, one track
Has been blown off; behind the butter-dish
Two Gunners kneel, whose gun has disappeared;
A Grenadier with busby and red coat
Mounts guard before a half a pound of cheese.
Some infantry with bayonets fixed begin
A slow advance towards the table edge.
Conscripted from another time and place
A wild Apache waves his tomahawk.
It's all a game. Upstairs, my youngest son
Roars like a little Stukka as he dives
Through dream, banks steep, then cuts his engines out,
Levels, re-enters the armistice of sleep.

VIEW FROM A DECKCHAIR

I rest in the canvas lap and let fall my book.
The breeze, browsing, flips a few pages,
Leaves it, then comes back for a second look.
My eyelids close, like mouths, on the images.

The sky is green with the smell of crunched grass
Whose dark, shed juice seasons the simmering air;
Eyelids slide open, eyes see a butterfly pass,
Pause, wings frittering, treading the air's water.

Summer mothers me; here I feel secure;
My neighbours are not likely to break down the fences;
The only guns they carry are for making war
On garden pests. Their televisions have valid licences.

Vapour-trails, squeezed out on the bland blue,
Perturb only slightly; the bee's buzz does not sting.
Even when a motorbike rasps in the avenue
The heart bucks only a little, and I stay sitting,

Or, rather, reclining in my garden chair,
And can stay here for at least another hour
Before the benevolent and grass-flavoured air
Loses its warmth, and the chill tastes sour.

END OF A SEASON

The nights are drawing in; the daylight dies
With more dispatch each evening;
Traffic draws lit beads
Across the bridge's abacus.
Below, black waters jitter in a breeze.
The air is not yet cold
But woven in its woof of various blues,
Whiffs of petrol and cremated flowers,
A cunning thread runs through,
A thin premonitory chill.
The parks are closed. Lights beckon from the bars.
The sporting news has put on heavier dress.
It is not autumn yet
Though summer will not fill
Attentive hearts again with its warm yes.

Far from the city, too, the dark surprises:
Oak and sycamore hunch
Under their loads of leaves;
Plump apples fall; the night devises
Frail webs to vein the sleek skin of the plums.
The scent of stars is cold.
The wheel-ruts stumble in the lane, are dry and hard.
Night is a nest for the unhatched cries of owls;
As deep mines clench their gold,
Night locks up autumn's voices in
The vaults of silence. Hedges are still shawled
With traveller's joy; yet windows of the inn
Rehearse a winter welcome.
Though tomorrow may be fine
Soon it will yield to night's swift drawing in.

The atheletes of light evenings hibernate;
Their whites are folded round

Green stains; the night
Reminds with its old merchandise –
Those summer remnants on its highest boughs –
That our late dancing days
Are doomed if not already under ground.
The playground gates are chained; the swings hang still,
The lovers have come down
From their deciduous hill;
Others may climb again, but they will not.
And yet the heart resumes its weightier burden
With small reluctance; fares
Towards Fall, and then beyond
To winter with whom none can fool or bargain.

STEVIE SMITH

STEVIE SMITH, who died in March 1971, was one of the
great eccentrics of contemporary English verse. A prolific
and entertaining writer, she was also a vigorous and captivating
performer of her own work, which she would sometimes
chant or sing to the tunes of popular psalms or traditional
English songs in a spell-brewing voice that was generally
(and memorably) off-key. In the last ten or so years of her life
she won for her work a growing audience which cut across
age-groups and the boundaries of the normal poetry-reading
public, and in 1969 she was awarded the Queen's Gold Medal
for poetry. This late success always struck her as ironic since
she was well into her thirties before she could find a publisher
willing to take on her poetry: even then, it was only after her
free-wheeling *Novel on Yellow Paper* had been hailed by the
critics as a remarkably original work.

Born in Hull in 1902, Stevie Smith was brought to London
when she was three by her mother and her aunt, settling in the
solid, heavily-furnished Palmer's Green house she was to
occupy for the rest of her life. She described that home in 'A
House of Mercy', a poem unusual both for its serious tone
and its autobiographical content, for in her verse Stevie Smith
generally hid herself away behind a regiment of wild, odd-
ball, scatty personas – some animal (cats, frogs, etc.), some
human. Her poems, in fact, have many faces. They can be
comical, absurd, whimsical, brooding, argumentative, melan-
cholic. But almost all have a directness which makes them
immediately accessible and a quality of voice and vision which

can be deceptively child-like. Indeed, her poems are hardly ever (the best of them anyway) what they seem – the vision of the child being directed by a hard and mature eye that could be cruel in its observation of human foibles and follies, the frolics of the clown being edged on occasions by a quite desperate sadness. 'Not Waving But Drowning' is perhaps the poem which conveys that desperation and sense of aloneness most completely and most perfectly, the tempo and tone of the verse carrying the shift in meaning and situation skilfully and, above all, naturally:

> Oh, no no no, it was too cold always
> (Still the dead one lay moaning)
> I was much too far out all my life
> And not waving but drowning.

There are then, as Stevie Smith herself has put it, 'different sorts of poems, you know, the argument poems, the melancholy ones, the ones about death and a tremendous lot about witchcraft and fairy poems, which I suppose are memories of childhood and Grimm's stories and the German fairy stories.' Nevertheless, there would seem to be one voice and one unifying personality behind all the kaleidoscopic faces and the sing-song, nursery-rhyme rhythms, behind all the banter and chatter. That personality has always struck me as being an essentially serious one seeking some kind of harmony or *modus vivendi* with the surrounding forces, be they those of Man, of Nature, or of God and the Christianity the poet fought a running battle with and finally rejected.

Formalized religion was certainly one of her prime targets, though sometimes her attack was slyly or ambiguously marshalled. As she characteristically wrote in *Novel on Yellow Paper*: 'Really, some of the people who go to church are just as good as those who stay away. But actually I am not a Christian actively. I mean I am actually not a Christian. I have a lot against Christianity though I cannot at the moment remember what it is.' Actually, of course, she remembered all too clearly, and in one of her 'argument' poems, 'Oh Christianity, Christianity', she spelt out her doubts precisely:

> You say He was born humble – but He was not,
> He was born God –
> Taking our nature upon Him. But then you say,
> He was Perfect Man. Do you mean
> Perfectly Man, meaning wholly: or Man without sin? Ah
> Perfect Man without sin is not what we are.

More than anything she loathed cant and superficiality, having little patience with those who lacked the courage to follow logic to its hard conclusions ('The Weak Monk'). She possessed that courage herself to a remarkable degree, as her last poem, 'Come Death' – written in hospital when she had lost the power of speech – nobly shows. Often over the years she had joked and flirted with death in her work, but as the reality of it approached she was its match, able to face it proudly, without self-pity, and with an almost Jacobean grandeur. In a fine late poem, 'Scorpion', she still held up the masks, approaching the subject artfully with her customary asides and fancies. In 'Come Death' there is no cover, and no illusion.

Because so many of Stevie Smith's poems are simply (or complexly) Comic, and may be pleasurably read and accepted on that level, one hesitates to emphasise the lonely, unsettling side of her questioning nature. Of course she disguised it often enough with a sleight of hand that was her great gift. One never knew the knife was going in until it was in, and often she accompanied her most 'serious' work with spikey, child-like drawings which kept the mood gay. She was never over-solemn, or pompous, or melodramatic, and those who were became immediate targets for her invective. Always she addressed her readers in a conversational tone which was in tune with her own manner of speaking, so that the Stevie of the printed page was very much the Stevie of the spoken word. If that was one source of her strength, it was a source of weakness also, for she could chatter prosaically and overlong, allowing her rhythms to slacken and her rhymes to slip. Sometimes, too, that chatter was not about very much.

Oddly, for someone so in tune with every-day gossip and speech, so excited and awed by the visible, terrible, absurdly human life around her, her work is sprinkled with classical and literary allusions. But the scholar is always servant to the poet's impish eye, and her literary characters are never allowed to take themselves seriously for long. Thus in a ridiculing or even self-mocking way she reduces everything to a common human denominator. She can be cruel in her observations, but she can be tender also, and one senses a heartfelt identification with, for instance, the pup-dog of her poem 'O Pug':

> O Pug, obstinate old nervous breakdown,
> In the midst of *so* much love,
> *And* such comfort,
> Still to feel unsafe and be afraid,
> How one's heart goes out to you!

The same is even true of such marvellous comic inventions as the 'Jungle Husband' and the newly weds of 'I Remember', and it makes them the more real. What is unusual too about such poems is the way the tone is controlled to catch *exactly* the innuendoes and speech rhythms of the human voice; it is this as much as anything else that gives the poems their flavour. One cannot but laugh with delighted recognition as The Jungle Husband writes:

You never want to go in a jungle pool
In the hot sun, it would be the act of a fool

Because it's always full of anacondas, Evelyn, not looking
   ill-fed
I'll say. . . .

John Wain has written that, 'What she felt and wrote and
imagined she *was*,' and that the most immediately striking
feature of her poetry was the perfect marriage of form and
content. 'She had a strong sense of the numinous' (he continued) 'that pervaded everything she wrote: she saw
humanity as rooted in nature, and she accepted nature with a
completeness that acknowledged its terrors and menaces as
well as its beauty and serenity. With unerring instinct she
found her own individual poetic vehicle for this vision: free-
running variable lines with strong rhymes, and a diction in
which the familiar and domestic took on an aureole of wonder
and, sometimes, of dread.'

More than anything it is the freshness and originality of her
vision one recalls most gratefully, together with the zest of her
writing. She has been compared to Blake, to Lear, to e. e.
cummings, to Thurber, but she was an original, going her
own way, singing her own strange songs.

————————

James MacGibbon writes:[1]

Stevie Smith, everyone would agree, was unique. It is not
within my scope or powers to define her position in English
poetry, but it seems to me that Sir Desmond MacCarthy's
comment some twenty-five years ago that she 'had a little
nugget of genius' is very happily confirmed by her inclusion
in this book, in a series edited by two contemporary poets, one
very young and the other by no means old. This is something
she would have enjoyed. It was the wide appreciation among

[1]Mr. MacGibbon, the distinguished publisher, was Stevie Smith's close
friend and is her literary executor.

old and young during the last five years of her life that must have enabled her, professionally speaking, to die happy. She was at the height of her fame at sixty-eight. I imagine she never had missed that fame when it was not offered, but she certainly savoured it to the full when it came; and in any case she had had, since the publication of her *Novel on Yellow Paper* in the mid-thirties, a hard core of appreciation within her own circle of friends and admirers.

All who read her poetry will recognize that death was no stranger to her: she had come to terms with her 'sweet and gentle friend' long ago, in a way that perhaps has not been so well understood by anyone since the seventeenth century. It is thus appropriate that the only poem that she left for posthumous publication, when she died harrowingly but tidily in March this year (1971), should be 'Come, Death'. It is appropriate too that it should first be read in this volume – one designed for a wide circulation.

When Stevie Smith lost her speech three weeks before she died as a result of brain cancer, she could still laugh. Hers was not nervous or embarrassing laughter of course. Life for her remained to the end a serious, tragic business but it never ceased to be funny – tragi-funny, in the manner of her famous poem, 'Not Waving But Drowning'.

One last personal word: I don't think that any of her friends, much though they loved her, thought of her as beautiful – she was so lively and quick one hadn't time anyway to take in much but her words. It was only when she was dying that a strikingly beautiful nobility became apparent. Perhaps that had something to do with her acceptance, unbeliever that she was, of death.

A HOUSE OF MERCY

It was a house of female habitation,
Two ladies fair inhabited the house,
And they were brave. For all though Fear knocked loud
Upon the door, and said he must come in,
They did not let him in.

There were also two feeble babes, two girls,
That Mrs. S. had by her husband had,
He soon left them and went away to sea,
Nor sent them money, nor came home again
Except to borrow back
Her Naval Officer's Wife's Allowance from Mrs. S.
Who gave it him at once, she thought she should.

There was also the ladies' aunt
And babes' great aunt, a Mrs. Martha Hearn Clode,
And she was elderly.
These ladies put their money all together
And so we lived.

I was the younger of the feeble babes
And when I was a child my mother died
And later Great Aunt Martha Hearn Clode died
And later still my sister went away.

Now I am old I tend my mother's sister
The noble aunt who so long tended us,
Faithful and True her name is. Tranquil.
Also Sardonic. And I tend the house.

It is a house of female habitation
A house expecting strength as it is strong
A house of aristocratic mould that looks apart
When tears fall; counts despair

Derisory. Yet it has kept us well. For all its faults,
If they are faults, of sternness and reserve,
It is a Being of warmth I think; at heart
A house of mercy.

THOUGHTS ABOUT THE PERSON FROM PORLOCK

Coleridge received the Person from Porlock
And ever after called him a curse,
Then why did he hurry to let him in?
He could have hid in the house.

It was not right of Coleridge in fact it was wrong
(But often we all do wrong)
As the truth is I think he was already stuck
With Kubla Khan.

He was weeping and wailing: I am finished, finished,
I shall never write another word of it,
When along comes the Person from Porlock
And takes the blame for it.

It was not right, it was wrong,
But often we all do wrong.

May we enquire the name of the Person from Porlock?
Why, Porson, didn't you know?
He lived at the bottom of Porlock Hill
So had a long way to go,

He wasn't much in the social sense
Though his grandmother was a Warlock,
One of the Rutlandshire ones I fancy
And nothing to do with Porlock,

And he lived at the bottom of the hill as I said
And had a cat named Flo,
And had a cat named Flo.

I long for the Person from Porlock
To bring my thoughts to an end,
I am becoming impatient to see him
I think of him as a friend.

(*Thoughts About the Person from Porlock cont.*)

Often I look out of the window
Often I run to the gate
I think, He will come this evening,
I think it is rather late.

I am hungry to be interrupted
For ever and ever amen
O Person from Porlock come quickly
And bring my thoughts to an end.

I felicitate the people who have a Person from Porlock
To break up everything and throw it away
Because then there will be nothing to keep them
And they need not stay.

Why do they grumble so much?
He comes like a benison
They should be glad he has not forgotten them
They might have had to go on.

These thoughts are depressing I know. They are depressing,
I wish I was more cheerful, it is more pleasant,
Also it is a duty, we should smile as well as submitting
To the purpose of One Above who is experimenting
With various mixtures of human character which goes best,
All is interesting for him it is exciting, but not for us.
There I go again. Smile, smile, and get some work to do
Then you will be practically unconscious without positively
. having to go.

THE WEAK MONK

The monk sat in his den,
He took the mighty pen
And wrote 'Of God and Men.'

One day the thought struck him
It was not according to Catholic doctrine;
His blood ran dim.

He wrote till he was ninety years old,
Then he shut the book with a clasp of gold
And buried it under the sheep fold.

He'd enjoyed it so much, he loved to plod,
And he thought he'd a right to expect that God
Would rescue his book alive from the sod.

Of course it rotted in the snow and rain;
No one will ever know now what he wrote of God and men.
For this the monk is to blame.

TENUOUS AND PRECARIOUS

Tenuous and Precarious
Were my guardians,
Precarious and Tenuous,
Two Romans.

My father was Hazardous,
Hazardous,
Dear old man,
Three Romans.

There was my brother Spurious,
Spurious Posthumous,
Spurious was Spurious,
Was four Romans.

My husband was Perfidious,
He was Perfidious,
Five Romans.

Surreptitious, our son,
Was Surreptitious,
He was six Romans.

Our cat Tedious
Still lives,
Count not Tedious
Yet.

My name is Finis,
Finis, Finis,
I am Finis,
Six, five, four, three, two,
One Roman,
Finis.

NOT WAVING BUT DROWNING

Nobody heard him, the dead man,
But still he lay moaning:
I was much further out than you thought
And not waving but drowning.

Poor chap, he always loved larking
And now he's dead
It must have been too cold for him his heart gave way,
They said.

Oh, no no no, it was too cold always
(Still the dead one lay moaning)
I was much too far out all my life
And not waving but drowning.

THE JUNGLE HUSBAND

Dearest Evelyn, I often think of you
Out with the guns in the jungle stew
Yesterday I hittapotamus
I put the measurements down for you but they got lost in
    the fuss
It's not a good thing to drink out here
You know, I've practically given it up dear.
Tomorrow I am going alone a long way
Into the jungle. It is all grey
But green on top
Only sometimes when a tree has fallen
The sun comes down plop, it is quite appalling.
You never want to go in a jungle pool
In the hot sun, it would be the act of a fool
Because it's always full of anacondas, Evelyn, not looking
    ill-fed
I'll say. So no more now, from your loving husband,
    Wilfred.

I REMEMBER

It was my bridal night I remember,
An old man of seventy-three
I lay with my young bride in my arms,
A girl with t.b.
It was wartime, and overhead
The Germans were making a particularly heavy raid on
   Hampstead.
What rendered the confusion worse, perversely
Our bombers had chosen that moment to set out for
   Germany.
Harry, do they ever collide?
I do not think it has ever happened,
Oh my bride, my bride.

OH CHRISTIANITY, CHRISTIANITY

Oh Christianity, Christianity,
Why do you not answer our difficulties?
If He was God He was not like us,
He could not lose.

Can Perfection be less than perfection?
Can the creator of the Devil be bested by him?
What can the temptation to possess the earth have meant to
   Him
Who made and possessed it? What do you mean?

And Sin, how could He take our sins upon Him? What
   does it mean?
To take sin upon one is not the same
As to have sin inside one and feel guilty.

It is horrible to feel guilty,
We feel guilty because we are.
Was He horrible? Did He feel guilty?

You say He was born humble – but He was not,
He was born God –
Taking our nature upon Him. But then you say,
He was Perfect Man. Do you mean
Perfectly Man, meaning wholly; or Man without sin? Ah
Perfect Man without sin is not what we are.

Do you mean He did not know that He was God,
Did not know He was the Second Person of the Trinity?
(Oh, if He knew this, and was,
It was a source of strength for Him we do not have)
But this theology of 'emptying' you preach sometimes –
That He emptied Himself of knowing He was God – seems
A theology of false appearances

To mock your facts, as He was God, whether He knew it
    or not.

Oh what do you mean, what do you mean?
You never answer our difficulties.

You say, Christianity, you say
That the Trinity is unchanging from eternity,
But then you say
At the incarnation He took
Our Manhood into the Godhead,
That did not have it before,
So it must have altered it,
Having it.

Oh what do you mean, what do you mean?
You never answer our questions.

O PUG!

O Pug, some people do not like you,
But I like you,
Some people say you do not breathe, you snore,
I don't mind,
One person says he is always conscious of your behind,
Is that your fault?

Your own people love you,
All the people in the family that owns you
Love you: Good pug, they cry, Happy pug,
Pug-come-for-a-walk.

You are an old dog now
And in all your life
You have never had a cause for a moment's anxiety,
Yet,
In those great eyes of yours,
Those liquid and protuberant orbs,
Lies the shadow of immense insecurity. There
Panic walks.

Yes, yes, *I* know,
When your mistress is with you,
When your master
Takes you upon his lap,
Just then, for a moment,
Almost you are not frightened.

But at heart you are frightened, you always have been.

O Pug, obstinate old nervous breakdown,
In the midst of *so* much love,
And such comfort,
Still to feel unsafe and be afraid,

How one's heart goes out to you!

SCORPION

'This night shall thy soul be required of thee'
My soul is never required of *me*
It always has to be somebody else of course
Will my soul be required of me tonight perhaps?

(I often wonder what it will be like
To have one's soul required of one
But all I can think of is the Out-Patients' Department –
'Are you Mrs. Briggs, dear?'
No, I am Scorpion.)

I should like my soul to be required of me, so as
To waft over grass till it comes to the blue sea
I am very fond of grass, I always have been, but there must
Be no cow, person or house to be seen.

Sea and *grass* must be quite empty
Other souls can find somewhere *else*.

O Lord God please come
And require the soul of thy Scorpion

Scorpion so wishes to be gone.

COME, DEATH

I feel ill. What can the matter be?
I'd ask God to have pity on me,
But I turn to the one I know, and say:
Come, Death, and carry me away.

Ah me, sweet Death, you are the only god
Who comes as a servant when he is called, you know,
Listen then to this sound I make, it is sharp,
Come Death.   Do not be slow.

TONY HARRISON

THE stir surrounding the publication of Tony Harrison's first full book of poems, *The Loiners* (1970), is understandable. Here at last was a young poet who had shown himself willing to be adventurous, to shun domesticity, to turn to other languages and literary traditions for his frames of reference, to match up to the demands of the permissive '70s without pandering to the whimsy of the Pop brigade. His work is not easy to pin down, his poems being a strange amalgam of intellect and primal energy, direct and illusive at one and the same time; they beat their own gongs loudly, yet are carefully worked, often over many pages and in strict verse forms.

The development from his early pamphlet, *Earthworks* (Northern House, 1964), is striking. Only one or two of those formal, run-of-the-mill early poems gave any indication of the large-scale, full-blooded work to come. The dramatic transformation has obviously been worked for, and in the newer work one senses a deliberate attempt to rough things up, to shock, to over-step the so-called bounds of 'good taste', to be as blatantly sexual as any film-maker, and as sensual. The sensual and tactile elements in art are clearly important to Harrison, as he made clear in an article on Cuba he wrote for *The London Magazine* (April, 1970): 'I am a chronic, inveterate feeler. I was once evicted from the *Musée de l'Art Moderne* for stroking Brancusi's *La Phoque*, which surely is what it was made for. Later in the National Gallery of Prague I discovered with the help of a Czech friend that if you carried a white stick, wore dark glasses, and took someone to guide you round, you could handle the extremities of the Rodins, and insinuate your connoisseur hand just wherever you wanted, even essay a bit of hesitant *frottage* if you fancied.'

This is only half the story, for clearly Harrison is a chronic thinker and an inveterate reader too, who enjoys confusing the issue by leading the reader down paths of specialized knowledge. Mostly, though, he writes about characters and places he knows or has known, about Leeds and its citizens (the 'Loiners' of his title), about Russia, Czechoslovakia, Africa – places where he has lived, taught, delved. A native of Leeds himself (he was born there in 1937, went to Leeds Grammar School, then to Leeds University where he read Classics), he brings to his Leeds poems a particular sense of period and place. The strength of these poems lies partly in the fact that their remembered heroes are out-of-the-way originals, partly in the honesty and exactness of the writing itself and the way it evokes one's own childhood memories and sense of loss. They are witty too, especially when things turn to sex, as in Harrison's work they so often do. In this respect, Peanuts Joe, the town's sexual Messiah, is among the most memorable of the Loiners, along with the more sober Thomas Campey (Books) who, 'in each demolished home, Cherished a Gibbon with a gilt-worked spine', and a strange cast of refugees and fumbling lovers.

The Leeds of Harrison's poems is clearly more than a symbol or framework; it is rather an organic part of the poetry itself. Even in an early autobiographical story, *The Toothache* (*Stand*, Vol. 5, No. 2), his deep-rooted attachment to the place comes through feelingly: 'He was nearer to his old home. You could see almost all of Leeds from the crest of Beeston Hill, the roofs, the chimneys and the steeples, the higher civic buildings, the clock of the black Town Hall, to which he had listened, in his attic bedroom, striking the small hours of those mornings immediately before he left. The slightest earth tremor could level them. He could see the familiar landmarks that he had passed on his way up. The Salem Institute, Hudson's Warehouse, formerly Wesley Hall, the gas cylinders, the truncated pinnacles of Christ Church. Some time ago, these had become insecure and the constant passage of heavy and rapidly increasing traffic had made them a danger to the community. The incumbent had sat for weeks at a trestle table, with placards ranged about him and fixed above the church porch on either side of what seemed to be a tinged photograph of Christ, beneath which was written in white capitals, COME UNTO ME. Who would go to that? . . .'

After leaving University, Harrison spent several years in Africa, immersing himself in the locale with the passion of the dedicated sociologist/anthropologist he undoubtedly is. A number of critics have hailed his long and ambitious African sequence, 'The White Queen', as his most impressive work to date. In the poem, Africa is seen through the eyes of two expatriate Loiners, an aging Public Works foreman and a homosexual professor. Peter Porter (in *The London Magazine*) personified that professor, speaking of him as 'that Greene-like collector of colonial absurdities who has put Somerset Maugham into bed with Petronius.' Porter continued: 'The exoticism is both shrewd and tender but gains most from a tropical freedom with words. The versification rocks on its narrow gauge but the scenery is wonderful.' The scenery is indeed wonderful, and there is vigour galore in the free-wheeling language, yet I must confess to finding the poem hard to accept *in toto* largely because the translations, epigrams and allusions Harrison introduces appear to me to clutter the narrative, drawing the poem on beyond its right length. It becomes, in fact, an intellectual jigsaw puzzle, the power and momentum of the opening giving way to something altogether more playful – like the 'Zeg-Zeg Postcards' he invents for the holidaying professor to send back from Europe.

Perhaps the Irish poet James Simmons was correct in saying

that the vivid and pointed observation of the Africa poems
make the smell and feel and look of Africa as real as Harrison's
Leeds and Newcastle scenes. Still, the Leeds poems, and the
more recent poem on Durham, strike me as being more central
to Harrison's vision that the African sequence, or even than his
engagingly direct Russian poems, which cleverly interweave
public and private themes, their message (as laid out in 'The
Bedbug') unambiguous:

> Comrade, with your finger on the playback switch,
> Listen carefully to each love-moan,
> And enter in the file which cry is real, and which
> A mere performance for your microphone.

That Comrade, travelling on Tony Harrison's 'Chopin
Express', would undoubtedly have had more to tune into
and observe than the poet's firm rhymes:

> The U.S. bit of sunlight knows
> I only have one cover – clothes.
> Enough conceits and epigrams!
> O let's knock back a few wee drams
> of warming vodka and/or rye,
> come to my sleeper, love, and lie,
> disarmed, defenceless, like a bride;
> we don't belong to either side.

One senses the spirit of Rimbaud in the air, urging the poet
towards a dare-devil cosmopolitanism; also, the hand of Robert
Lowell, casting a restraining shadow. In Tony Harrison's
best work, these energies and disciplines converge to cross-
fertilize his wide and colourful interests with his inventive
talent. He has said that he is 'worried to the point of madness
by punishment and love'. In 'The Nuptial Torches' one sees
this concern explored within an historical context and with

dazzling panache; in 'Fonte Luminosa' the approach is less direct but verbally and conceptually no less exciting. In both cases the Dionysian drive has been matched by technical excellence. If such successes have to be paid for by occasional lapses of taste and excursions into rhetoric, then the price would seem well worth the paying.

————————

Tony Harrison writes:

When I search my childhood for something to explain what drove me into poetry, something like Pablo Neruda's story of the silent exchange of a toy lamb and a pine cone between himself and an unseen boy through a hole in a fence, I can find nothing quite so significantly beautiful, but there are things which brought to me, early but obscurely, the same precious idea 'that all humanity is somehow together.' 'To feel', Neruda says, 'the affection that comes from those unknown to us who are watching over our sleep and solitude . . . widens out the boundaries of our being and unites all living things!, My images are all to do with the War. One of my very earliest memories is of bombs falling, the windows shaking, myself and my mother crouching in the cellar listening, me begging to be allowed to rush out into the lit-up streets, the whistlings sounded so festive. The next morning I found the overgrown tennis courts in the local park pitted with bomb craters. As I rooted around in one for shrapnel, I heard someone talking to a policeman utter the still haunting but no longer so puzzling phrase: *humane bomber.* Another is the contact I had with German prisoners of war in a work party near our street. I remember only we children talked to them much. I introduced them to the pleasures of smoking cinnamon sticks, and bought their supplies from the chemist. Another is of a street party with a bonfire and such joy, celebration and general fraternity as I have never seen since. As I grew up the

image stayed but I came to realize that the cause of the celebration was Hiroshima. Another is the dazed feeling of being
led by the hand from a cinema into the sunlit City Square
after seeing films of Belsen in 1945, when I was eight. Around
all these too is a general atmosphere of the inarticulate and
unmentionable, a silence compounded of the hand-me-down
Victorian adage, 'children should be seen and not heard' and
the mock-Yorkshire taciturnity of 'hear all, see all, say nowt.'
Even now when I have finished a poem I have bouts of
speechlessness in which that fireside atmosphere again casts
dark shadows in my skull. When I began my travels, I con-
verted that into a third part of my small-time self dramatiz-
ations of 'silence, exile and cunning.'

In our street in Hoggarty Leeds I was the only one who used
his literacy to read books, the only 'scholar', and so every
kind of cultural throwaway from spring-cleaned attics and
the cellars of the deceased found its way to me. I acquired
piles of old 78's, George Formby, the Savoy Orpheans,
Sophie Tucker, Sandy Powell, Peter Dawson, and sometimes
the odd book, an old guide to Matlock, the *Heckmondwike
Temperance Hymnal* stamped *Not To Be Taken Away*, and,
above all, a Livingstone's *Travels* so massive I could barely
manhandle it. Somehow it seems that my two early ambitions
to be Dr. Livingstone and George Formby, were compromised
in the role of poet, half missionary, half comic, Bible and
banjolele, the Renaissance *ut doceat, ut placeat*.

Although there were strenuous and exhausting years under
formal education, my vividest memories of enthralled
achievement are in minor closet dramas of midnight or dawn
autodidacticism in the style of Thomas Cooper the Chartist
poet. In some ways I still re-enact this when I write a poem.
My school, Leeds Grammar School, to which I won one of
six scholarships for the plebs, seemed to me like a class
conspiracy. When I left my final report said: 'He possesses
something of the poetical imagination, but suffers from the

waywardness of that gift.' The windows behind the altar in the school chapel were dedicated to *Miles*, the soldier, and *Mercator*, the merchant. Somehow I can't recall the pig in the middle. But when I close my eyes now I see *Poeta*, the poet, sometimes as poised, saintly and acceptable as his worldly flankers, sometimes like some half-naked shaker in the throes of a virulent *scribendi cacoethes*, being belaboured by public school angels wielding gamma minuses like immense shillelaghs over their glossy Cherry Blossomy hairstyles, driving the poet from the Garden of Eton.

It was probably no less a pressure than the whole weight of the Protestant Ethic in its death agonies, a monstrous North of England millstone grit, that made me pit myself against the most difficult traditional verse forms. It had to be hard work, and it was, and it still is. I learned by what Yeats called 'sedentary toil and the imitation of great masters.' I still find it all almost impossibly difficult, but the difference is now that, again in the words of Yeats, 'difficulty is our plough.' Nothing encourages me more than the progress from a first to a final draft in Yeats. Some of my poems in *The Loiners* went through as many as 40 or 50 versions. The forms I taught myself, through use and an enormous amount of translation, none of which I kept, are now enactments of unresolved existential problems, of personal energies in ambiguous conflict with the stereotype, sexual, racial, political, national. The themes, like Zarate's History of Peru, are about discovery *and* conquest; celebration and defeat.

The myth of Virgil, whose *Aeneid* I read and re-read for some five years and still read often, and whose laborious mother-bear methods of composition I adopted as a heroic posture of my own, is a constant threat to the most hubristic poetic self-confidence. Virgil asked for his 'botched' epic to be burned at his death. The example of Rimbaud is also disturbing. Fracastorius, part of whose *Syphilis* (Verona, 1530) I translated in *The Loiners* was born literally without a mouth and died speechless. And there is that most haunting epigraph in the whole of literature, the sentence from Azedinne El Mocadecci, prefixed to Edward Powys Mathers' masterly and beautiful rendering of the Panchasika of Chauras, *Black Marigolds*: 'And sometimes we look to the end of the tale that there should be marriage feasts, and find only, as it were, black marigolds and a silence.' With these examples in mind and haunted by recent history on which speech gags, the choice, especially in an environment where poetry was only for the 'lassy-lad', seemed to lie between making my poetry important against all odds or giving it up, renouncing all this fiddle for the more important thing. I can't see myself achieving the first, and however hard I try, I don't seem to be able to manage the second, so I expect that like Virgil I'll put off the final renunciation until my deathbed. Meanwhile I go on trying, wavering between a parody of heroic effort I learned in the hushed attic of my childhood, and an equally mock heroic vow of silence.

The Loiners (citizens of Leeds, *citizens* who bear their loins through the terrors of life, 'loners') was begun in Africa, after I had thawed out my tongue on a Nigerian version of the *Lysistrata*, which I translated and adapted with James Simmons, the Irish poet. Shortly after the publication of *The Loiners*, I was killing time in Hereford Cathedral before catching a train home after giving a reading from the book, and suddenly I found myself standing before the *Mappa Mundi*, a thirteenth century map of the world like a golden brain with a tumour somewhere near Paradise. If you look at Africa on it, you see all its prodigies, the Hermaphrodites, the Himantopodes, the four-eyed Marmini, the Psylli, the Troglodytes, and the kin of Fracastorius the mouthless race of Ethiopia and all their strange brothers. But in great gold letters the Dark Continent is labelled EUROPE. Prebendary A. L. Moir, writing on this incredible error, suggests either that the names were added erroneously by a later hand, or, and I like to think that this is the truth, that it is 'an attempt to represent Africa–Europe as a single entity with interchangeable names.' I felt the same almost unbearable excitement staring at the *Mappa Mundi* (with no New World as yet) as I felt when I first read the words of Thomas Browne which I use as an epigraph to the African poems in *The Loiners*: 'There is all Africa and her prodigies in us; we are that bold and adventurous piece of nature.' Or when about to move to Newcastle-upon-Tyne, where I am now living, after four years in Africa and a year in Prague, I read in a poem attributed to John Cleveland:

Correct your maps: Newcastle is Peru.

That accident (I had my head split open by a laundry van at the age of three), *that accident, Mrs. 'Arrison,* I overheard a neighbour say to my mother, *all that there reading. It'll turn 'is 'ead.* Now I hear her saying: *I told you so.*

THE HANDS

All his hopes were hands, his ventures hands,
all hands; hands no less crucial, no less lithe
than a desperate climber's or a drowning man's,
on swollen silks and bulging velveteens
ran sideways on, stopped, slithered off, gained ground
again, then flopped like frogs into a pond
and surfaced white and weightless like dead frogs.

And all the wine they hurried back and forth
for warmth into his mouth was but a drop
in all the coastless oceans that they pushed
or scooped or drifted on, until they caught
an instant on a breast or thigh, or skulked
from hostility in some rank hair and scuttled off,
sensing injury if they but stopped for breath.

Left to themselves again while others paired
or nested gently on sweet hair, his crept away,
albino things abandoned of their kind;
crouched quivering on his face. He flung them down.
They bunched in terror from this savage beast.

They say that afterwards the pair of them
were huddled on the parapet and he
gazed at them hard, half lovingly, half cold,
like a man at kittens he is going to drown.

He dropped them twitching in the cold canal.

Heavily weighted, they struggled well,
kicking up the water, then went down.

THOMAS CAMPEY
AND THE COPERNICAN SYSTEM

The other day all thirty shillings' worth
Of painfully collected waste was blown
Off the heavy handcart high above the earth,
And scattered paper whirled around the town.

The earth turns round to face the sun in March,
he said, resigned, *it's bound to cause a breeze.*
Familiar last straws. His back's strained arch
Questioned the stiff balance of his knees.

Thomas Campey, who, in each demolished home,
Cherished a Gibbon with a gilt-worked spine,
Spengler and Mommsen, and a huge, black tome
With Latin titles for his own decline:

Tabes dorsalis; veins like flex, like fused
And knotted flex, with a cart on the cobbled road,
He drags for life old clothing, used
Lectern bibles and cracked Copeland Spode,

Marie Corelli, Ouida and Hall Caine
And texts from Patience Strong in tortoise frames.
And every pound of this dead weight is pain
To Thomas Campey (Books) who often dreams

Of angels in white crinolines all dressed
To kill, of God as Queen Victoria who grabs
Him by the scruff and shoves his body pressed
Quite straight again under St. Anne's slabs.

And round Victoria Regina the Most High
Swathed in luminous smokes like factories,

These angels serried in a dark, Leeds sky
Chanting *Angina-a, Angina Pectoris.*

Keen winter is the worst time for his back,
Squeezed lungs and damaged heart; just one
More sharp turn of the earth, those knees will crack
And he will turn his warped spine on the sun.

Leeds! Offer thanks to that Imperial Host
Squat on its thrones of Ormus and of Ind,
For bringing Thomas from his world of dust
To dust, and leisure of the simplest kind.

THE NUPTIAL TORCHES

These human victims, chained and burning at the stake, were the blazing torches which lighted the monarch to his nuptial couch.
— J. L. Motley, *The Rise of the Dutch Republic*

Fish gnaw the Flushing capons, hauled from fleeced
Lutheran Holland, for tomorrow's feast.
The Netherlandish lengths, the Dutch heirlooms,
That might have graced my movements and my groom's
Fade on the fat sea's bellies where they hung
Like cover-sluts. Flesh, wet linen wrung
Bone dry in a washerwoman's raw, red,
Twisting hands, bed-clothes off a lovers' bed,
Falls off the chains. At Valladollid
It fell, flesh crumpled like a coverlid.

Young Carlos de Sessa stripped was good
For a girl to look at and he spat like wood
Green from the orchards for the cooking pots.
Flames ravelled up his flesh into dry knots
And he cried at the King: *How can you stare
On such agonies and not turn a hair?*
The King was cool: *My friend, I'd drag the logs
Out to the stake for my own son, let dogs
Get at his testes for his sins; auto-da-fés
Owe no paternity to evil ways.*
Cabrera leans against the throne, guffaws
And jots down to the Court's applause
Yet another of the King's *bon mots.*

O yellow piddle in fresh fallen snow —
Dogs on the Guadarramas . . . dogs. Their souls
Splut through their pores like porridge holes.
They wear their skins like cast-offs. Their skin grows
Puckered round the knees like rumpled hose.

Doctor Ponce de la Fuente, you,
Whose gaudy, straw-stuffed effigy in lieu
Of members hacked up in the prison, burns
Here now, one sacking arm drops off, one turns
A stubble finger and your skull still croons
Lascivious catches and indecent tunes;
And croaks: *Ashes to ashes, dust to dust.*
Pray God be with you in your lust.
And God immediately is, but such a one
Whose skin stinks like a herring in the sun,
Huge from confinement in a filthy gaol,
Crushing the hooping on my farthingale.

O Holy Mother, Holy Mother, Ho-
ly Mother Church, whose melodious, low
Labour-moans go through me as you bear
These pitch-stained children to the upper air,
Let them lie still tonight, no crowding smoke
Condensing back to men float in and poke
Their charcoaled fingers at our bed, and let
Me be his pleasure, though Philip sweat
At his rhythms and use those hateful tricks
They say he feels like after heretics.

O let the King be gentle and not loom
Like Torquemada in the torture room,
Those wiry Spanish hairs, these nuptial nights,
Crackling like lit tapers in his tights,
His seed like water spluttered off hot stone.
Maria, whose dark eyes very like my own
Shine on such consummations, Maria bless
My Philip just this once with gentleness.

The King's cool knuckles on my smoky hair!

Mare Mediterraneum, la mer, la mer
That almost got him in your gorge with sides
Of feastmeats, you must flush this scared bride's
Uterus with scouring salt. O cure and cool
The scorching birthmarks of his branding-tool.

Sweat chills my small breasts and limp hands.

They curled like foetuses, *maman*, and cried.

His crusted tunics crumple as he stands:

Come, Isabella. God *is satisfied.*

NEWCASTLE IS PERU

Correct your maps: Newcastle is Peru!
— John Cleveland

Venient annis saecula seris,
Quibus Oceanus vincula rerum
Laxet & ingens pateat tellus,
Tethysque novos detegat orbes,
Nec sit terris ultima Thule.

— Seneca, *Medea*, 375–9

For defending in our Civil Wars
the King's against the better cause,
Newcastle got its motto: FORTIT-
ER TRIUMPHANS DEFENDIT.
After Nigeria and Prague I come
back near to where I started from,
all my defences broken down
on nine or ten *Newcastle Brown.*

A sudden, stiff September breeze
blows off the sea along the quays
and chills us; autumn and I need
your shoulder with a desperate need.
A clumsy effort at control,
I faff with paper chips and coal,
and rake out with elaborate fuss
one whole summer's detritus.

A good draught and the fire roars
like muted Disney dinosaurs,
and last week's Sunday paper glows
yellowish, its urgent prose,
like flies across a carcass, spreads

and fattens on the voiceless dead.
A picture shows lobbed mortar bombs
smashing down Onitsha homes.

The fire sucks in the first cold air
under the coverage of massacre.
The fire chatters, almost flies,
a full-fledged bird of paradise.
I lay down, dizzy, drunk, alone,
life circling life like the Eddystone
dark sea, but lighting nothing; sense
nor centre, nor circumference.

A life-long, sick sixpennyworth
of appalling motion round the Earth;
scared, moonrocketing till Pop –
eye and blurred planets stop;
Switchback; Helter Skelter; Reel;
the Blackpool Pleasure Beach Big Wheel,
its million coloured lightbulbs one
red halo like an empty sun.

The *Caterpillar; Hunslet Feast;*
one hand on my first woman's breast;
darkness; acceleration so
we're desperate with vertigo;
then chained in solitary *Chair-*
o-planes through whistling air
as all the known Leeds landmarks blur
to something dark and circular.

Venus, Vulcan, Cupid stare
out vacantly on City Square,
and *Deus iuvat impigros*
above the bank where God helps those

who help themselves, declares
Leeds purposeful in its affairs.
Mercator; miles, school chapel glass
transparencies to blood and brass.

And *Self Help* Samuel Smiles was said
to have waltzed round our first bed
in our partitioned ballroom flat
with hardly room to swing a cat.
Worthies! Loiners! O King Dick
Oastler and his rhetoric,
and William Hey, the first to show
syphilis *in utero.*

O highlife crocodiles that went
round one palm tree in the bare cement!
The dizziness! That spiral stair
up St. Vitus's Cathedral; there
the golden cockerel and great Prague
before us like a catalogue;
slides. Bloodless mementos, all
Time-Life International.

And now with vistas like Earl Grey's
I look out over life and praise
from my unsteady, sea-view plinth
each dark turn of the labyrinth
that might like a river suddenly
wind its widening banks into the sea
and Newcastle is Newcastle is Newcastle *is* Peru!

Swirled detritus and driftwood pass
in state the 1880 *Sas-
inena Cold Storage Co.,*

and Neptune gazes at the Tyne's flow
seawards, where the sea-winds 'boast
and bluster' at the North East coast,
the sluggish Tyne meandering through
the staithes and shipyards of Peru.

Shadow girders faced with sun
shimmer like heaped bullion.
Commerce and contraceptives glide
and circle on the turning tide;
Plain, *Gossamer* and *Fetherlite*
and U.S. *Trojan*, knotted tight,
ferry their unborn semen, free
for ever from discovery.

Discovery! Slaves, now trains,
like *spirochetes* through dark brains,
tunnel the Andes, spiralling for zinc
and silver, gold and lead; drink
still makes me giddy; my mind whirls
through all my wanderings and girls
to one last city, whose black crest
shows all the universe at rest.

At rest! That last red flash
as life's last ember turns to ash
and riddled dusts drop through the grate
around the heart. O celebrate,
as panic screws up each charged nerve
to cornering the next sharp swerve,
Earth, people, planets, as they move
with all the gravity of love.

First this Victorian terrace, where
small scars of the last World War –

those wrought iron railings made
into shrapnel and grenade,
acanthus leaf and fleur-de-lys,
victorious artillery –
are enough reminder that we brave
harsh opposition when we love.

This cluttered room, its chandelier
still spinning from the evening's beer,
this poor, embattled fortress, this strong-
hold of love, that can't last long
against the world's bold cannonade
of loveless warfare and cold trade,
this bed, this fire, and lastly us,
naked, bold, adventurous.

Discovery! wart, mole, spot,
like outcrops on a snowfield, dot
these slopes of flesh my fingers ski
with circular dexterity.
This moment when my hand strays
your body like an endless maze,
returning and returning, you,
O you; you also are Peru.

And just as distant. Flashing stars
drop to the ashpit through the bars.
I'm back in Africa, at ease
under the splashed shade of four trees,
watching a muscled woman heave
huge headloads of dead wood; one bare leaf
for covering wilts in the heat,
curls, then flutters to her flat, cracked feet.

And round each complex of thatched huts

is a man-high cactus hedge that shuts
out intruders and the mortars thud
like a migraine in the compound mud.
Night comes, and as drunk as hell
I watch the heavens and fireflies, and can't tell,
here at my Shangri-la, Pankshin,
where insects end and stars begin.

My fingerprints still lined with coal
send cold shudders through my soul.
Each whorl, my love-, my long life-line,
mine, inalienably mine,
lead off my body as they press
onwards into nothingness.
I see my grimy fingers smudge
everything they feel or touch.

The fire I laid and lit to draw
you downstairs to the second floor,
flickers and struts upon my bed.
And I'm left gazing at a full-page spread
of aggressively fine bosoms, nude
and tanned almost to *négritude*,
in the Colour Supplement's *Test
Yourself for Cancer of the Breast.*

A PROPER CAUTION

The sun's in cloud. The fat man with string-vest
Patterns sun-printed on his woman's chest,
Starts up from his deck chair suddenly,
And dragging his toe-ends in the ebbing sea,
Crowned with a useless *Kiss Me*, King Canute,
Red-conked and ludicrous, but still a man,
Shouts out before the cuddlesome and cute
To death and a darkness: *Stop!* to prove they ran.

DURHAM

'St. Cuthbert's shrine
founded 999'
(*Mnemonic*)

ANARCHY and GROW YOUR OWN
whitewashed onto crumbling stone
fade in the drizzle. There's a man
handcuffed to warders in a black sedan.
A butcher dumps a sodden sack
of sheep pelts off his bloodied back,
then hangs the morning's killing out,
cup-cum-muzzle on each snout.

I've watched where this 'distinguished see'
takes off into infinity,
among transistor antennae,
and student smokers getting high,
and visiting Norwegian choirs
in raptures over Durham's spires,
lifers, rapists, thieves, ant-size,
circle and circle at their exercise.

And Quasimodo's bird's-eye view
of big wigs and their retinue,
a five car Rolls-Royce motorcade
of judgement draped in Town Hall braid,
I've watched the golden maces sweep
from courtroom to the Castle keep,
through winding Durham, the elect
before whom ids must genuflect.

But some stay standing and at one
God's irritating carrillon
brings you to me; I feel like the hunch-

back taking you for lunch;
then bed. All afternoon two church-
high prison helicopters search
for escapees down by the Wear
and seem as though they're coming here.

Listen! Their choppers guillotine
all the enemies there've ever been
of Church and State, including me,
for taking this small liberty.
Liberal, lover, communist,
Czechoslovakia, Cuba, grist,
grist for the power-driven mill
weltering in overkill.

And England? Quiet Durham? Threat
smokes off our lives like steam off wet
subsidences when summer rain
drenches the workings. You complain
that the machinery of sudden death,
Fascism, the hot bad breath
of Powers down small countries' necks
shouldn't interfere with sex.

They *are* sex, dear, we must include
all these in love's beatitude.
Bad weather and the public mess
drive us to private tenderness,
though I wonder if together we,
alone two hours, can ever be
love's anti-bodies in the sick,
sick body politic.

At best we're medieval masons, skilled
but anonymous within our guild,

at worst defendants hooded in a car
charged with something sinister.
On the *status quo*'s huge edifice
we're just excrescences that kiss,
cathedral gargoyles that obtrude
their acts of 'moral turpitude'.

But turpitude still keeps me warm
in foul weather as I head for home
down New Elvet, through the town,
past the butcher closing down,
hearing the belfrey jumble time
out over Durham. As I climb
rain blankets the pithills, mist
the chalkings of the anarchist.

I wait for the six-five Plymouth train
glowering at Durham. First rain,
then hail, like teeth spit from a skull,
then fog obliterate it. As we pull
out of the station through the dusk and fog,
there, lighting up, is Durham, dog
chasing its own cropped tail,
University, Cathedral, Gaol.

Walking on the Great North Road
with my back towards London
through showers of watery sleet,
my cracked rubber boot soles
croak like African bullfrogs
and the buses and lorries that swish
like a whiplash laid on and on
without intermission or backswing
send a spray splashing over
from squelching tyres skywards
STOP red, GO green, CAUTION
amber, and at the crossing
where you had your legs crushed
I remember the *fonte luminosa*,
Brasilia's musical geyser
spurting a polychrome plumage,
the fans of rich pashas,
a dancer's dyed ostriches,
making parked Chevrolets
glisten, people seem sweaty,
and when yellowing, loppy Therezinha,
the eldest, though your age,
of the children all huddled
under the fancy ramp entrance
of the National Theatre,
comes and scoops from the churned
illuminated waters a tinful
for drinking and cooking and goes
gingerly to ingenious roads
where cars need never once
stop at Belishas or crossings,
intersect, crash, or slow down,
the drops that she scatters

are not still orange or purple,
still greenish or gorgeous
in any way, or still gushing,
but slightly clouded like quartz,
and at once they're sucked back
into Brazil like a whelk
retracting, like the tear
that drains back into your eye
as once more you start coming through
the rainbowing spindrift and fountains
of your seventh anaesthesia.

DANIEL HOFFMAN

DANIEL HOFFMAN was born in New York City in 1923, served in the U.S. Air Force from 1943–46, has taught at various American and European universities and is now Professor of English at the University of Pennsylvania. The first of his five published books of poems, *An Armada of Thirty Wales*, appeared in 1953 in the Yale Series of Younger Poets – the choice of W. H. Auden, who wrote a six-page Foreword to the volume. In it, Auden dwelt on the problems of writing 'Nature poetry' in an increasingly technological civilization. 'The poet today', he wrote, 'is faced not only with the question of contemporary expression but also with the task of recovering the feeling which he and the public have largely lost, that Nature is numinous. He has to make a much more conscious and deliberate effort.'

As Auden pointed out, Daniel Hoffman sought to tackle this problem by exact observation and description rather than by pretending to some Wordsworthian intimacy with Nature. Yet his involvement then with what Auden called 'the frontier between earth and water, and with the creatures associated with it,' was neither literary nor photographic, as both 'The Clams' and 'The Seals in Penobscot Bay' show. In 'The Clams', the tug and force of nature is communicated directly so that the reader is drawn into the poem and involved:

> All shrinks in the rage of the sun
>   save the courage of clams, and their faith:
>
> Sacrificing the water they breathe
>   seems to urge the tall moon from her orbit;

she tugs oceans cubit by cubit
over killdeer's kingdom

and ends parched freedom.

In 'The Seals in Penobscot Bay' the physical presence of the
seals themselves is conveyed strongly, and yet this is only the
poem's starting point, the verse moving both eye and mind
towards another arena as the reference to Odysseus and the
Sirens is worked in – Odysseus who, to escape the luring
enchantment of the Siren's songs and the death they har-
boured, ordered his crew to block their ears with wax and
then to lash him firmly to the mast.

In the course of his next four books, Hoffman edged slowly
away from the matter and style of his early work to en-
compass the city and its attendant landscapes, as well as other
specifically 'modern' involvements and preoccupations. The
gradual refinement of his technique and the movement
towards an *apparent* impersonality is deceptive. Often one
has to move back into a poem carefully after the initial reading
to discover its pulse, only perceiving then the degree to which
form and content have been fused. Most impressive is his
ability to work on several levels simultaneously, to shift
emphasis in the course of a poem, to transform unpromising,
fairly prosaic material into something memorable. In 'In the
Beginning', for instance, the scene set in the opening lines is
ordinary enough; but as father and daughter stand watching
the sea-spray, the associations begin their mysterious work:

> Her ecstasy's contagion
> touches the whirling gulls
>
> and turns their gibbering calls
> to 'Boat! Boat!' Her passion
>
> to name the nameless pulls her
> from the syllabic sea.

One senses the subject gradually taking hold of the poet, the symbolic significance of the experience reaching into the unconscious to open up areas and possibilities which raise the poem to an altogether different level:

> That verbal imagination
> I've envied, and long wished for:
>
> The world without description
> is vast and wild as death ...

All the time, though, Hoffman retains contact with the real situation sketched in the opening lines, branching from it and returning to it on cue. The poem thus maintains both its sense of reality and its unity, while at the same time setting up reverberations and echoes.

The same happens in 'Safari', where the flat opening (it could have come from some instruction manual) speeds one unknowingly towards the encounter between boy and snake, the muscle of the verse tightening from the fourth line on as those of the kneeling boy were to do. The poet has withdrawn, or is there only in the recalled experience, careful not to over-strain the effects – and at the right moment he brings the poem back onto even keel, breaking the spell with the mother's sharp interjection:

> To do what with those creatures?
> You'll drown them in the drain at once!

That encounter with 'numinous nature' is recalled on a colloquial as much as on a 'poetic' level, and the same may be said of many of Hoffman's most successful poems. When he lapses (as on occasions he does) it is because either the poetic or the colloquial have gained the upper hand – in the one case over-rarifying the experience, in the other offering it up too readily. In the best poems, the language is elegant yet in tune with the spoken voice, the metaphors right, the stanzas tightly controlled and containing their subject in a way which heightens the tension and dramatic impact. Generally, too, the perception is sharp, as is the mind which steers the subtle arguing. 'Daniel Hoffman is an observer' wrote Marianne Moore, 'and what he finds the rhythm does not contradict. He "thinks" – and what he thinks has substance.'

The refinement of diction, the gradual paring down of the verse to its verbal minimum, is shown to good effect in 'A Meeting' (from Daniel Hoffman's third book, *The City of Satisfactions*, 1961):

> He had awaited me,
> The jackal-headed.
>
> He from Alexandria
> In the days of the Dynasts,
>
> I from Philadelphia
> In a time of indecisions.

The poem is a triumph of taste, the fascinating interplay between the animate and the inanimate, the observer and the agate-eyed observed, being perfectly captured by the relaxed, springy rhythms and the casual tone. It is with some surprise that one finds oneself in the British Museum, amidst references to mythology and the wrecks of earlier civilizations. The poem shifts gear skilfully, the quiet wit of the originally-slanted opening being matched and balanced by the warm lyricism of the closing stanzas with their carefully cast rhymes and half-rhymes. Commenting on this poem in his book *Alone with America*, Richard Howard wrote: 'It is wonderful that this poet's reserves of feeling are always stirred to intensest life by the fictive, the hieratic, and that his imagination of forms is fired most by the ritual, the legendary, the profoundly *impersonal*.' This is not always (or not only) so. 'The Pursued' (from the same volume) moves, for example, into territory that is altogether more Kafkaesque, and it can be no coincidence that one of the three poets Hoffman focused on in his critical book *Barbarous Knowledge* was Edwin Muir, who translated Kafka into English. Indeed, the three poets of that book (Muir, W. B. Yeats and Robert Graves) have all left something of themselves on Hoffman's work, and it is revealing to read his poem 'Key' with his remarks on Robert Graves' poem 'Warning to Children' in mind. 'In a dreamlike iteration and reiteration', wrote Hoffman, 'he admonishes them to beware of unwrapping the appearances of things, for appearance encloses appearance in boxes within boxes.'

In Daniel Hoffman's more recent work, the hidden threats, the mysterious pursuers, the surrealistic juxtaposing of images, the landscapes of terror, return – though not exclusively, and not always as directly as in 'The Pursued'. There is also tenderness ('Last Words') and a growing social involvement ('A Special Train'). In the love poem 'Last Words', he attains a rare level of feeling and communion by speaking naturally and working from the concrete. In 'A Special Train', where the subject is ostensibly less personal, the method used is not dissimilar, while the areas of feeling he opens up are every bit as genuine. That 'Special Train' moves mechanically through its unnamed Oriental landscape (Vietnam), but the poet's empathy with the victim creates a peculiarly nightmarish atmosphere so that finally it is not the train one remembers but the smeared hands, the back flecked with ash, the boy's moan which becomes an accusatory scream in the poet's head. One comes to understand why Richard Eberhart called Hoffman one of the best American poets of his generation, and to see the justness of his remark that, 'from his strong restraints burst dazzling powers.'

Daniel Hoffman writes:

I appreciate the invitation to comment on my own work, though I am diffident to comply. For who can do this without seeming pretentious, and anyway shouldn't one's poems simply speak for themselves with neither prolegomenon nor annotation? Still, an American author in a British anthology may, I trust, be indulged in a few explanations. For we all know that a common language, like a border, may as readily divide as join the peoples who share it.

When in London a few years ago, I attended meetings of a group of poets who discussed each others' work. On one occasion the poems on the agenda were mine. I recall that a passage describing a still sky bisected by the trail of a jet plane occasioned comments that surprised me.

> The halves of heaven
> Are bluer than each other,

my poem claimed. In the U.S. such a seminar would likely have considered the technical aspects of the poem – consistency of diction, handling of images, the rhythmic assumptions beneath the movement of the language. But in that intense circle off Earl's Court Square, debate centered instead upon the truth or falsity of the statement. It was the moral character of the speaker of the words in the poem which engaged the discussants. 'It's not possible,' one maintained, 'for one half of the heavens to be a different shade of blue from the other half.' I was dumbfounded, for I knew the proposition to be true; I had tried faithfully to record my own experience.

A few months later, back in Pennsylvania, I read the same poem and asked the same question of my daughter's class in the local high school. These sixteen year-olds restored my confidence as a teller of unambiguous truths. 'Of course it's true,' said one girl, 'because the part of the sky you are looking at is always bluer to you than the part you aren't.' Try it, and you'll see. But then, how much opportunity to experience the sky's variable blue does a reader have whose life is spent in hopes of 'bright intervals'?

Such misunderstandings are easily mitigated by simple explanations. There's another, graver difficulty for an American poet's work (it is mine of which I speak) set loose among British readers. With the best will in the world those readers tend, I suspect, to approach any American poet in terms of certain *idées reçues* about America. If such readers think of American literature at all, without their necessarily having ever read Philip Rahv's essay on the subject they will likely assume the truth of his division of our writers into two camps. In their imaginations they will see the palefaces (Hawthorne and Henry James, in *their* imaginations taking tea among a clutter of inherited European *meubles*) and, in the other camp, yawping around the open fire, the redskins ('Walt Whitman am I – one of the roughs – of Manahatta the son'). Such readers prefer that American poets be redskins.

Yet only a decade ago most would have thought Eliot the major poet of this century. But now that Eliot is dead and William Carlos Williams has at last been published in England, these readers have discovered the American anti-Establishment, the Pound-Williams-Beat-and-Black Mountain strains, without, it would seem, realizing that the anti-Establishment has quickly become a new Establishment and has produced its own academicism. But what are they to make of the American poet who writes neither beat nor projective verse, and is an enthusiast of neither the breath line nor the drug culture? Nor does he repudiate all manner for the sake of the 'deep image', nor all matter for compulsory confessions.

My poems have other concerns than these, yet are written in response to the very circumstances which seem propitious for the movements I do not choose to join. Let them respond in their ways and I in mine; in the house of poetry there are many mansions. Our country is farther along the way which industrial capitalism, technology and bureaucracy make inevitable for all developed nations. For us, these pressures towards monolithic social structures are exacerbated by our traditions of individualism. Two incompatible tendencies tear us apart. There is everywhere, for men and women of feeling, an unequal struggle between their institutions and their freedom. The energy of our poetry results from our living and writing under such pressures.

'If I am overflowing with life, am rich in experience for which I lack expression, then nature will be my language full of poetry – all nature will *fable*, and every natural phenomenon be a myth.' Thoreau wrote this in his journal, and I believe in it with him. The myth of which he speaks is not a tale from a vanished pantheon but the design of our own lives, the interplay of the constants of the life pattern with the varying circumstances of individual and cultural experience. I have always been intrigued by the connections between instinct and custom, ritual and dream. Much of my reading has explored these connections in folklore, and in the literature of psychology and anthropology – as may be inferred from some of my poems and from the titles of two of my critical studies (*Form and Fable in American Fiction* and *Barbarous Knowledge: Myth in the Poetry of Yeats, Graves, and Muir*). In prose I've been driven to explore such connections in the work of past writers, in verse by the need to discover their persistence in ourselves.

Auden, in his generous foreword to my first book, speaks of the difficulty of being a poet of nature in the twentieth century. I didn't undertake to write such poetry because of its difficulty, but because I then felt, and feel still, that the man who responds to the world of creatures, primal energies and rhythms is in touch with the sources of our own nature. A poet's obligation should be to restore to the center of life the numinous objects, relationships, and feelings menaced by the mechanism of mass society which, if we let it, would reduce us all to mere transistors in a huge computer, whirring not for the sake of men and women but for Mammon and power.

For all that, I resist being ticketed as either a poet of nature or a poet of myth. One can't help but hold in imagination, as in one's hands, the intractible realities of the day. In my last book, *Broken Laws*, are poems whose speakers have broken the laws of nature or our lesser laws. Among them are a citizen co-opted against his will in a war waged by his government; and a scientist whose pursuit of knowledge has fallen out in ashes. There is an assassin who confuses the leader he envies with the God he hates; there is a thief; a groundling in a space age; and a dreamer afraid to awaken to reality from his nightmare. Poems in *Striking the Stones* describe the industrial landscape 'whose archetypes/Have not yet been dreamed'; others measure my city, Philadelphia, against the promise of its founder William Penn, whose statue atop City Hall dominates the skyline. The title poem in *The City of Satisfactions* retells, as in a Western, the pursuit and loss of that elusive treasure, the Great American Dream.

Some contemporaries respond to the exigency of the times by making anew the repudiations of the modernists of 1912. Half a century later we may not so blithely get along without the imagination of historical experience. Poetry must be born from inner necessity. Because political institutions seem inflexible, some would make of poetry a fragmentation grenade to blast sensibility apart; but inner necessity may speak of the continuities and repetitions of our experiences, as much as proclaiming the uniqueness of our sufferings now. I do not believe that the history of the race, the language, or the art never were, or became obsolete when I got the vote. Nor do I find the necessity of intrinsic form as a tensor of meaning in poetry a deprivation of one of my natural rights.

If the culture seems in the throes of a nervous breakdown, some poets will exacerbate the symptoms of its affliction. Others will be driven back upon their own resources. In the celebration of love, in the revelation of the instinctual rhythms of feeling, in the discovery of the movements the mind makes in reassembling the dry bones of the broken world into a living unity, such poets may help us to define our humanity.

I've been speaking, of course, of the kind of poems I'd like to write; for those I have written thus far, all I dare hope is that some readers may take pleasure in them.

THE CLAMS

In the Bay of Fundy the clams
lie stranded, half-dry, by the tides

forty feet higher than sea
in killdeer's kingdom.

Underground, they erect valved snouts.
Wet freckles sprout over the beach:

Each trickles a droplet, and each
attests to the desperate hope

that attends each ritual drop.
Lie ten-hours-buried in sand

and the swirl of salt and the wet
seems an Age before suffering began.

All shrinks in the rage of the sun
save the courage of clams, and their faith:

Sacrificing the water they breathe
seems to urge the tall moon from her orbit;

she tugs ocean, cubit by cubit
over killdeer's kingdom

and ends parched freedom.
Moon, with sky-arching shell

and bright snout nine thousand miles long
and anemones in her kelp hair

that gleam in the heaven around her,
responds with the wave of their prayers

or sucks the sea unawares.

THE SEALS IN PENOBSCOT BAY

hadn't heard of the atom bomb,
so I shouted a warning to them.

Our destroyer (on trial run) slid by
the rocks where they gamboled and played;

they must have misunderstood,
or perhaps not one of them heard

me over the engines and tides.
As I watched them over our wake

I saw their sleek skins in the sun
ripple, light-flecked, on the rock,

plunge, bubbling, into the brine,
and couple & laugh in the troughs

between the waves' whitecaps and froth.
Then the males clambered clumsily up

and lustily crowed like seacocks,
sure that their prowess held thrall

all the sharks, other seals, and seagulls.
And daintily flipped the females,

seawenches with musical tails;
each looked at the Atlantic as

though it were her looking-glass.
If my warning had ever been heard

it was sound none would now ever heed.
And I, while I watched those far seals,

tasted honey that buzzed in my ears
and saw, out to windward, the sails

of an obsolete ship with banked oars
that swept like two combs through the spray.

And I wished for a vacuum of wax
to ward away all those strange sounds,

yet I envied the sweet agony
of him who was tied to the mast,

when the boom, when the boom, when the boom
of guns punched dark holes in the sky.

IN THE BEGINNING

On the jetty, our fingers shading
incandescent sky and sea,

my daughter stands with me.
'Boat! Boat!' she cries, her voice

in the current of speech cascading
with recognition's joys.

'Boat!' she cries; in spindrift
bobbling sales diminish,

but Kate's a joyous spendthrift
of her language's resources.

Her ecstasy's contagion
touches the whirling gulls

and turns their gibbering calls
to 'Boat! Boat!' Her passion

to name the nameless pulls her
from the syllabic sea.

She points beyond the jetty
where the uncontested sun

wimples the wakeless water
and cries, 'Boat!' though there is none.

But that makes no difference to Katy,
atingle with vision and word;

and why do I doubt that the harbor,
in the inner design of truth,

is speckled with tops'ls and spinnakers,
creased with the hulls of sloops?

Kate's word names the vision
that's hers; I try to share.

That verbal imagination
I've envied, and long wished for:

the world without description
is vast and wild as death;

the word the tongue has spoken
creates the world and truth.

Child, magician, poet
by incantation rule;

their frenzy's spell unbroken
defines the topgallant soul.

SAFARI

You need an empty burlap
bag; rubber boots;
a forked longhandled stick.
You need nerves like roots

of the willow half underwater
that stiffen the trunk they grip
though that trunk hold boughs aquiver
at the quietest breath.

You kneel on the willow's knees
probing the fern-rimmed ditch
till an arrow furrows the water,
till quiet is cleft by hiss

and quick and true the sinew
tightens in your arm, in your throat
and true and quick the long stick
lunges: a thunderbolt

pinions the diamond head
where the forking tongue is set
immobilizing nothing
else of that undulant jet –

I see those brave safaris
and my triumphal returns,
the writhing bag that dangles
from the forked stick's horns,

that dangles over the rosebuds
staked to the trellis I passed,
home through the tender garden
my prize held fast

– 'To do *what* with those creatures?
You'll drown them in the drain at once!' – and dream
of a boy, rigid, goggling
down the manhole's gloom

at serpents hugely striding
in the diamonded darkness agleam
and thrashing the still black waters
till they foam and rise like cream.

A MEETING

He had awaited me,
The jackal-headed.

He from Alexandria
In the days of the Dynasts,

I from Philadelphia
In a time of indecisions.

His nose sniffed, impassive,
Dust of the aeons.

A sneeze wrenched my brain
– I couldn't control it.

His hairy ears listen
Long. He is patient.

I sift tunes from the winds
That blast my quick head.

His agate eye gazes
Straight ahead, straight ahead.

Mine watch clocks and turn
In especial toward one face.

I thank Priestess of Rā
Who brought us together,

Stone-cutters of Pharaoh
And The Trustees of

The British Museum.
When with dog-eared Anubis

I must sail toward the sun
The glistening Phoenix

Will ride on our prow;
Behind the hound-voices

Of harrying geese
Sink the cities of striving,

The fiefdoms of change
With which we have done,

Grown in grandeur more strange,
More heroic than life was

Or the dark stream at peace,
Or wings singed in the sun.

THE PURSUED

Surely he'd outwitted them, outdistanced them and earned
Respite at this café. There goes the ferry.
Two trips risked in his own person, over
And back, and now, in this wig
Crossed again. Nobody knew him.
Coffee under the arbor, mission done,
Content. And then he recognized
The first signs –
Heat, hotter than the day's heat, swarming
And his skin parched, stretching
Tight about each finger; the eyes
Pounding: arbor, harbor,
Table, gable, all begin to swing
Up and forth, forth and up, up and so, until
Giddily earth grinds beneath him, shudders;
Sweat oozes icy on his neck now,
On shaking chest a shirt of seaweed crawls,
Iron table rat-tat-tat-tat-tats against his elbow
Though harbor's calm and arbor's still. You've seen
A stepped-on centipede left on the pavement,
Each limb's oracular gesticulations?
– Cutting through the scent of pear trees
Klaxons, baying, toil up up the highroad,
Vans of his other pursuers.

KEYS

As the days grow shorter many keys
Hang from our chains –
Keys to boxes, drawers, trunks, and rooms
Filled with trunks and drawers
And boxes, keys to vaults and keys to houses,
Heavy keys of wrought-iron, filed
To fit the doors we can't remember closing.
Keys that seem unlike our own
Keys that we would open gates with.
Walking through the aery corridors and gates
Ever ajar,
The road ahead unbarred and open
– See, if we turn
Around, the way lies
Behind us. We could go
Back down the very lanes we've been
Where nothing's changed,
Had we the one
Key that doesn't
Hang from these heavy chains.

MOVING AMONG THE CREATURES

Moving among the creatures
As the new light
Surges down this cliff, these trees, this meadow,
Brightening the shade among the alders
And shrivelling the dew on leaves,
They are contented in their bodies – I can tell it –
The squalling gulls delighted to be turning
Widdershins, their shadows swooping
Over rocks where startled deer
Clatter, flashing spindly shanks
And delicate hooves while underfoot
Even the uglies in their sticky skins
Exult, the woodfrogs clunking all the bells
In sunken steeples, till at my
Thick tread
They leap and scissor-kick away
While the withering leech,
Shrinking, enlarging, waving
Knobbed horns
Makes the stem shine
With silver spittle where he's gone.
I trip on vines, stumble in potholes
And long for something of myself that's in them,
In the gulls' windy coursing, in the frogs'
Brief cadenza, even in the slug's
Gift to leave
A gleaming track, spun
From his own
Slippery gut.

LAST WORDS

Eleven o'clock. It's time
I made my will. To you,
Musebaby, I leave
These jottings.

What will you do with them?

They are of no earthly use,
And you deserve, require
A goodly world of looking-after –
I'd fit you out

With the whole kit and garterbelt,
Gowns, togas, suits, capote,
Any hat you choose; a house
With miracle kitchen, an antique

Butcher's table, and perfume,
Bath-oil, a carved four-poster
With a featherbed and tester,
A daughter and a son,

Life insurance, car – the lot.
It's a life I'd give you.
How can I leave it with you?
Where go without you?

That would be nowhere, no life,
Nothing like the bits and pieces
Of the life that's in these scribblings
I make because of you.

Though little good they do you
You don't care, you needn't
You are yourself, it's you I need
And all I leave are but the ways

I've found of saying so

A SPECIAL TRAIN

Banners! Bunting! The engine throbs
In waves of heat, a stifling glare
Tinges the observation-car

And there, leaning over the railing,
What am I
Doing in the Orient?

Blackflies, shrapnel-thick, make bullocks
Twitch. The peasants stand
Still as shrines,

And look, in this paddy
A little boy is putting in the shoots.
He's naked in the sunlight. It's my son!

There he is again, in that
Field where the earth-walls meet.
It's his play-time. See, his hands are smeared

With mud, and now his white
Back is flecked with ash, is seared
By embers dropping from the sky –

The train chuffs past. I cry
Stop! Stop! We cross another paddy,
He's there, he's fallen in the mud, he moans my name.

SELECTED BIBLIOGRAPHY

THOMAS HARDY:
Collected Poems (Macmillan & Co.)
The Life of Thomas Hardy by Florence Emily Hardy (Macmillan & Co.)
Thomas Hardy by Edmund Blunden (Macmillan & Co., 1942; Macmillan paperback, 1967)
Thomas Hardy by Douglas Brown (Longmans, Green, 1953)
'Mr. Hardy's New Poems' – a *New Statesman* review of December 19, 1914 by Lytton Strachey included in *Characters and Commentaries* (Chatto & Windus).
See also, *New Bearings in English Poetry* by F. R. Leavis (Chatto & Windus, 1938).

DANNIE ABSE:
Tenants of the House (Hutchinson, 1957)
Poems, Golders Green (Hutchinson, 1964)
A Small Desperation (Hutchinson, 1968)
Selected Poems (Hutchinson, 1970; New York, Oxford University Press, 1970)
Three Questor Plays (Scorpion Press, 1967)
O. Jones, O. Jones (Fiction: Hutchinson, 1970)
Ash On a Young Man's Sleeve (Autobiographical novel, 1954; republished by Vallentine, Mitchell, 1970)
A critical article on Dannie Abse's work by Roland Mathias appears in *The Anglo-Welsh Review* (Winter, 1967). For a statement by Abse on his own work see the *Poetry Book Society Bulletin* (London, Summer 1964); for interviews, the *Jewish Quarterly* (London, Winter 1964) and *Twentieth Century* Magazine (No. 10034, 1963, and No. 1036, 1968).

VERNON SCANNELL:
A Sense of Danger (Putnam, 1962)
Walking Wounded (Eyre & Spottiswoode, 1968)
Epithets of War (Eyre & Spottiswoode, 1969)
Selected Poems (Allison & Busby, 1971)

The Tiger and the Rose (Autobiography; Hamish Hamilton, 1971). An interview with Vernon Scannell appears in *The Poet Speaks* (Routledge, 1966) and a 'Profile' in *The Guardian* of August 10, 1970. For an assessment of his work by Anthony Thwaite, see *Contemporary Poets of the English Language* (St. James Press, 1970).

STEVIE SMITH:

Not Waving But Drowning (André Deutsch, 1957)

Selected Poems (Longmans, Green, 1964)

The Frog Prince (Longmans, Green, 1966)

Scorpion and Other Poems (Longmans, Green, 1971)

Novel On Yellow Paper (Jonathan Cape, 1936)

A statement by Stevie Smith on her own work may be found in *X Magazine*, eds. David Wright and Patrick Swift (Volume 1: published by Barrie and Rockliff, 1961), and an interview with her is included in *The Poet Speaks* (Routledge, 1966). For a review by David Wright of *Not Waving But Drowning* see *Poetry Chicago* (August, 1958), and for an article on her work by D. J. Enright ('Did Nobody Teach You?') see *Encounter* (June, 1971).

TONY HARRISON:

Earthworks (Northern House Pamphlet, 1964)

The Loiners (London Magazine Editions, 1970)

A review of the *Loiners* by Peter Porter appeared in *The London Magazine* (September, 1970), and an essay on Tony Harrison's work by James Simmons in *The Honest Ulsterman* (Sept./Oct., 1970). Tony Harrison's article on Cuba – 'Shango the Shanky Fairy' (London Magazine, April 1970) – throws interesting light on the poetry.

DANIEL HOFFMAN:

A Little Geste (New York, Oxford University Press, 1960)

The City of Satisfactions (New York, Oxford University Press, 1963)

Striking the Stones (New York, Oxford University Press, 1968)

Broken Laws (New York, Oxford University Press, 1970)

Form and Fable in American Fiction (Criticism: New York, Oxford University Press, 1961)

Barbarous Knowledge: Myth in the Poetry of Yeats, Graves and Muir (Criticism: New York, Oxford University Press, 1970)

Richard Howard includes a chapter on Daniel Hoffman's work in his book *Alone with America* (London, Thames & Hudson, 1970). An article on Hoffman's work by William Sylvester appears in the American magazine *Voyage* (Winter, 1970) and an interview (with W. B. Patrick) in *Pennsylvania Review* (No. 3, 1971).